COMMON-SENSE TIME MANAGEMENT FOR PERSONAL SUCCESS

COMMON-SENSE TIME MANAGEMENT FOR PERSONAL SUCCESS

Barrie Pearson

Livingstone Fisher Plc

MERCURY

First published in hardback in 1988 by Mercury Books
Reprinted November 1990

Reprinted in paperback November 1991
by Mercury Books, Gold Arrow Publications Ltd,
862 Garratt Lane, London SW17 0NB

Set in Plantin and Univers by Phoenix Photosetting
Printed and bound in Great Britain by
Mackays of Chatham PLC, Chatham, Kent

Cartoons by Ken Pyne

British Library Cataloguing in Publication Data

Pearson, Barrie
    Common-sense time management for personal success.
    1. Business firms. Personnel. Personal
    success. Achievement. Applications of time
    allocation
    I. Title
    650.1

ISBN 1-85252-094-9

To Catherine

My reason for managing time effectively is
to enable me to enjoy as much time as
possible with her

PREFACE

There are countless books on time management. Unfortunately, time management is merely a valuable aid to personal success, and not a recipe for it.

This book is first and foremost about personal success. Time management is covered in detail, but not as a goal in itself. You cannot consider time effectively in isolation, but only in relation to the achievement of specific goals.

Equally, there is no merit in efficiency unless it contributes significantly to the achievement of a chosen goal. For many people, work is comfortable, rewarding and enjoyable. Unfortunately, work is often the enemy of achievement. The most effective way of doing certain tasks may well be to deliberately leave them undone, because they have a minimal effect upon the achievement of a particular goal.

One factory I visited has a large sign on the wall which read 'never confuse movement and action'. Your personal motto should be a variation on this theme, namely 'never confuse work and results'. You know that this has the ring of truth about it. Some people achieve success seemingly effortlessly and enjoyably, whilst many people struggle endlessly only to end up still struggling. The choice is up to you.

This book spells out the ingredients for success. The crucial first step is to choose consciously the kind of success you want. Sadly, many people simply do not know what they want and so success will happen to them only by fortunate accident. When you know what you want, then you need to believe you *will* achieve it and you must want to achieve it very badly. This is still not enough to ensure success. Action is essential to translate your vision and belief into reality. This book is designed to make success happen for you.

You must focus and harness your energies to make success happen for you. Even so, this is still not enough. You must persuade, motivate and influence other people to contribute towards and share in your success. So effective time management is vital because success requires more than doing tasks effectively and efficiently. Time must be found to persuade, motivate and influence people as well.

Fortunately, every person is given the same amount of time each day. Time is your most precious resource, and in this respect you are the equal of the most successful people who have ever lived. Forget the idea that education and money determine success, they merely affect where you start from.

Success requires balance in your life, otherwise sooner or later it may prove barren and futile. Examples make this obvious. What is 'success' if you lose your health, or your spouse, or your children, or end up without friends in the process of achieving it? So by all means focus on success, but don't pursue it to the detriment of the other things in your life which may suddenly matter more to you if you ever lose them.

This book has been written primarily to help you achieve personal success in the fields of business, management and career progress. Nonetheless, the principles described are fundamental to the achievement of success at any time and in any sphere of your life.

There is an old saying: 'Tomorrow is the first day of the rest of your life.' If you are *really* serious about success, this isn't good enough. You should think instead, 'Today is the first day of the rest of my successful life.' So act now, by reading Chapter 1!

A special thank you is appropriate to Anne Garay, who not only typed the manuscript, but contributed to the chapter on the role of a personal assistant.

Livingstone Fisher Plc,   BARRIE PEARSON
Acre House, 11–15 William Road,
London NW1 3ER

CONTENTS

COMMON-SENSE TIME MANAGEMENT FOR PERSONAL SUCCESS

1 | HOW TO DECIDE WHAT SUCCESS YOU REALLY WANT

When you have read this chapter, *and implemented it*, you will:

- have decided what personal success you want to achieve

- have defined your *personal vision* of success goals

- have adopted the quantum leap approach to success

- believe you will achieve success

- focus on achieving your success goals

- be undeterred by setbacks

- recognise what else you *need* to achieve to enjoy your success

- have realised that these are the crucial elements necessary to achieving personal success

Success is entirely personal, highly subjective and relative. It is what you want. If you want to run your own small business, then that by definition is success. Someone else may wish to become the chief executive of one of the world's 500 largest companies. This is *not* a greater success than running your own business, if that is what you *really* want.

The prerequisite of achieving success for most of us is to consciously decide what success we do want for ourselves. If you know what success you want, but it is not happening quickly enough for you or you don't even know where to start to make it happen – fine! The rest of this book will help you to overcome these problems.

So many people simply do not know what success they want or have never bothered to think about it consciously, perhaps because they take a 'what will be, will be' approach to life. This is nonsense, and totally unnecessary. Worse still, some people have the attitude that knowing what they want won't make a jot of difference to them; the worst will still happen. This is tantamount to inviting the worst to happen, and then being proved 'right' when it does. Reject any such negative approach. Be positive. Decide what you really want. Start to do it now. 'But,' I hear you saying to yourself, 'if only I knew where and how to start.'

Well, start off by remembering the words of the song – 'accentuate the positive'. Answer the following questions for yourself:

- What things am I good at?
- What kinds of business would I like to work in or to own?
- What are my assets?

Answering these simple questions will point you in the right direction to head towards success; consider them for a moment with a little imagination. For example imagine you are an assistant manager in a branch of a bank who wants to escape from banking.

What things am I good at?

The skills you have developed in your job which could be valuable outside banking may include:

- handling customers
- supervising staff
- book-keeping
- a knowledge of mortgages, personal pensions and insurance

All of us have additional skills, which may be even more valuable to our future success than the ones we have learned during our career, for example:

- experience as a yachtsman and qualified navigator
- fluency in French

What do I enjoy doing, or would enjoy given the chance?

Your answers may be:

- dealing with people
- everything to do with boats and sailing
- being a salesperson (and having a company car)
- using my knowledge of mortgages, personal pensions and insurance

What kinds of business would I like to work in or to own?

Possible answers for this person include:

- a company connected with virtually any aspect of boats and sailing
- the financial services industry other than banking

What are my assets?

Money and financial assets are not the only ones which are needed and helpful for success. People whom you know may be invaluable. Either you, a relative, or a friend may know someone who could help you get that vital break. If you intend to set up your own business, then your personal contacts may well be a valuable source of potential custom, advice and help.

Knowledge you have may be an asset that you have never stopped to consider and yet may provide attractive opportunities for you. For example, if you have worked in the Far East for some years in a particular industry, when you return to your home country to live, your knowledge of the area could be valuable to a company wishing to set up an importing business. Equally, opportunities to become self-employed or to start your own business often arise from knowledge you have gained as part of your job. All that is required is for you to manage your time to make enough time to consider the opportunities which are available to you. For example, the job of a management development executive of a multinational company was to choose short external training courses for managers to attend and to organise internal training courses using a lot of external speakers and consultants. Using the knowledge acquired in this way, this person today owns a small business helping companies to organise tailor-made training programmes for their own staff.

As well as accentuating the positive it pays to eliminate the negative, so another question to be answered is:

What work, situations, frustrations and stresses do I wish to avoid?

For someone wishing to get out of banking, the answer may include commuting to a major city, never getting out of the office, lots of boring paperwork and the same routines repeated every day.

You may still be sat there thinking, 'This sort of thing only happens for other people.' It happens for people who regard themselves as ordinary because they help it to happen. A woman in her fifties was an administration manager and wanted to get off the five day a week treadmill, but she still needed to earn a living. She *managed her time* to research local opportunities to use her skills as a talented cook. One of her assets was that she lived in an area where people were willing to pay for someone to prepare food for their dinner parties and to deliver it to their homes. She now works only two or three days a week, earns more money and, most importantly, enjoys her work which she finds fulfilling. Time management not only enabled her to have the time to identify the opportunity, but allowed her to test the potential success before giving up a well-paid job. She mentioned the service to friends and acquaintances, then took days of holiday to handle the first few orders to be sure that sufficient demand existed at a price which would make the service financially worthwhile. This illustrates that an essential part of time management is to choose what things you need to do, and not simply do what you already do more efficiently.

Now is the time for action. Today is the first day of the rest of your successful life. Writing things down on paper is an effective way to think clearly. So take time now to complete the self-assessment questionnaire on the following pages. Write in pencil, so that you can change and refine your ideas. When you have completed it, look at it again tomorrow because more thoughts may come to you when you start to think in this way.

Self-assessment questionnaire

1. What things am I good at?

2. What do I enjoy doing, or would enjoy given the chance?

3. What kinds of business would I like to work in or to own?

4. What are my assets?

5. What work situations, frustrations and stresses do I wish to avoid?

The self-assessment questionnaire is designed to make you take stock of your own potential for success and to consider the ways you can achieve success. This gives you the opportunity to decide what success you want, and not merely manage your time better doing something you would prefer not to be doing anyway.

Having decided on the kind of success you want, the next step is to write down your success goals. Answer these two questions for yourself.

- What goal(s) will I achieve within three years?

- What goal(s) will I achieve within one year?

Timescales of one and three years allow you to choose major goals to be achieved. This brings perspective and focus to your time management. It enables you to identify the vital things which must be done and to plan the time and locate the resources to do them.

Consider a sales person selling industrial products in her own sales territory who wishes to continue working for her present company provided she achieves adequate career progress.

What goal(s) will I achieve within three years?

- To become a district sales manager

In order to obtain this success, relevant sub-goals need to be identified and achieved. Some of these may require an investment of time in the immediate future which is not to your best advantage in the short term. Effective time management requires making the time available to do what is important. Relevant sub-goals may include:

- To become one of the most successful salespeople within the company.

- To demonstrate the ability to win new customers and to sell new products successfully.

- To help provide product knowledge and sales training for new sales-people, because this will demonstrate your managerial potential even though it will reduce the time available to you for selling to customers.

What goal(s) will I achieve within one year?

Your one-year goals will be partly defined by your three-year goal because they will materially contribute to achieving it. So the one-year goals needed to help the salesperson become a district manager within three years may be:

- To become one of the top ten salespeople within the company in terms of:
  - total value of orders won
  - number of new customers obtained
  - sales of new products which are launched

Without going into more detail, it is important to define the sub-goals which will help achieve the one-year goal.

You may be thinking, 'I have already got the job I want, the problem is that I have been told my performance is barely adequate.' If this is the case, depending upon how urgently you need to demonstrate an improvement in your performance in order to achieve your goal of keeping your job, you may wish to change the timescales to, say, three months and one year. The key is to choose timescales which are relevant to the achievement of your success goals.

Whatever the timescale you choose, however, defining sub-goals is important to achieve your success goals. If your performance is not up to standard, then it is essential to define the important sub-goals which will bring a dramatic improvement.

Take action now. Complete the success goal questionnaire. Again, work in pencil and review your sub-goals occasionally. Be ready to add, delete or amend sub-goals from time to time if a change in circumstances requires a different approach to achieve the overall goals.

Three-year success goals

The goal(s) I will achieve within three years are:

Sub-goals which need to be achieved are:

One-year success goals

The goal(s) I will achieve within one year are:

Sub-goals which need to be achieved are:

Adopt the quantum leap approach to success

Surprisingly often, no more time or effort is required to achieve a dramatic increase in success than to produce a modest improvement. The outcome depends to a large extent on what level you set your sights on. The choice is up to you.

The quantum leap approach means that you consciously set goals which require a dramatic increase in your success. There is nothing wrong with, and a lot to be said in favour of, setting extremely demanding success goals. If you do so, however, it is even more important to define the sub-goals which must be achieved along the way. To achieve success goals of quantum leap proportions you must focus your energies on what is important.

If you already own your own business or are employed as chief executive of a company, then the quantum leap approach is especially relevant for you. Some examples are:

- to triple or quadruple profits within three years
- to become the market leader in your business sector within five years by a combination of organic growth and acquiring other companies
- to expand your company dramatically in order to obtain a stock exchange listing within four years
- to enter the temporary office staff market in the USA and to become the market leader within the medium term by acquiring two or three major companies
- to achieve a management buy-out of your subsidiary company within the next year

The quantum leap approach often proves to be highly motivating for staff and encourages everyone to focus on producing outstanding results rather than simply doing work.

Now that you have become aware of the quantum leap approach, there is no better time to start adopting it than *now*. So review your success goals and decide whether they are sufficiently demanding and rewarding. If you have not adopted the quantum leap approach enough when you set them, then rewrite them by setting your sights higher.

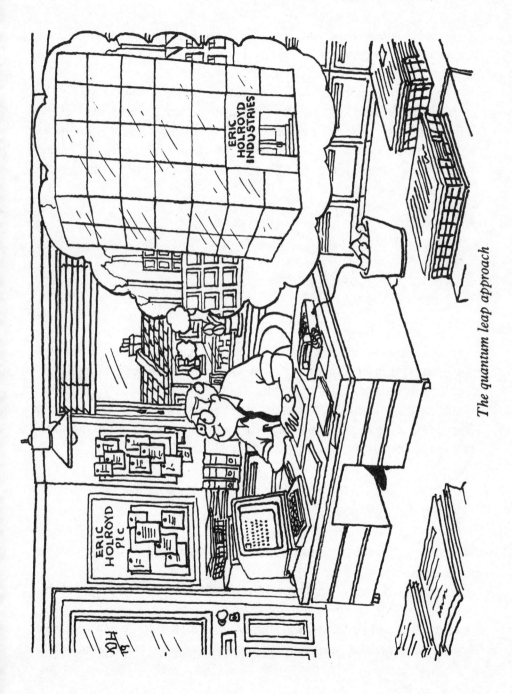

The quantum leap approach

Believe in the power of belief

You must *believe* that your success goals are achievable within the timescale you have set and *believe deeply* that you can and will achieve them.

Idle dreaming will not achieve your success goals. *Fortunately, the power of belief and effective time management will.* Belief implies the holding of a deep-rooted conviction, which is based on facts, evidence and plans. To develop and reinforce your belief that you will achieve your success goals, you need to complete the following statements.

My success goals

- are important to me because
- are achievable because
- the obstacles to be overcome are
- the priorities to focus on are

In completing these statements, it is important to think as clearly as possible. An example may be helpful to you to illustrate what is required. Consider someone who owns a chain of estate agents which he has built up into six branches over a seven-year period. By adopting a quantum leap approach, he has decided to create a regional network of at least forty branches within three years and to bring the company to the stock market within this period. His answers could be:

My success goals are important to me because

- my family and I will become financially independent for the rest of our lives
- my burning ambition is to bring a company to the stock market
- I would like my staff to have capital reward for their hard work and loyalty to me

My success goals are achievable because

- the management team has the ability and ambition to manage a much larger business than at present

- we have identified the towns in which we will either open a branch or acquire an existing business

- an insurance company has offered to buy a minority equity stake in the business and to provide rapid finance for expansion

The obstacles to be overcome are

- we do not have a qualified finance director, which is highly desirable for a stock market listing

- our auditors are unsuitable for a company intending to get a stock market listing

- we need to computerise urgently to be able to cope with dramatic expansion in the number of branches

The priorities to focus on are

- creating a programme for opening new branches and achieving it

- promoting the most capable branch managers to become area managers so that motivation and control of the branches is maintained

- recruiting an outstanding financial director capable of achieving the computerisation required and directing a programme to prepare the company for obtaining a stock market listing

Developing answers in a meaningful way as illustrated above provides a sound basis for believing that the success goals will be achieved. So the next step is for you to complete the following questionnaire.

Reasons for achieving success

My success goals are important to me because:

My success goals are achievable because:

The obstacles to be overcome are:

The priorities to focus on are:

Having completed the questionnaire, you now know what your priorities are and the obstacles and setbacks you may face. This means that you will have the resolve and the determination to overcome any obstacle or setback by anticipating them, wherever possible, and finding a way around them.

Achieve balance in your life

You need to achieve some degree of balance in your life otherwise you may achieve your success goals only to find you have lost what you belatedly discover is more important to you.

Time management used effectively means that you will not just find time, but plan time, for the things which are essential for you to enjoy success.

Your health

This requires you to pay attention to what you eat and how much alcohol you drink. Equally important, you must plan and make time available for exercise and relaxation. If your health suffers, your success may simply lead to bitterness.

Your family and friends

It is so easy to enjoy work so much and to focus so much on your success goals that you feel you don't really 'need' to spend much time with your family. You are providing them with plenty of money to do the things they enjoy. Don't fool yourself. Otherwise, you may end up in the divorce courts, find yourself seeing little of your children when they have grown up, or have few friends and acquaintances outside of work. The gift your family and friends value and appreciate most is spending time with you, when you have temporarily left thoughts of work behind you.

Something to consider in order to achieve balance in your life is to get involved with helping the community or working for a charity. If you can choose an activity which you can be involved in with members of your family, so much the better. Who knows, you may meet someone who can help you achieve your success goals.

How to decide the success you really want – action checklist

By now, you should have:

- completed a self-assessment to identify what you are good at; what you enjoy and would enjoy; what kind of business makes sense for you; what are your *real 'assets'*; and what you wish to avoid

- defined your success goals to focus on the *important* things to be achieved; set three-year and one-year success goals; identified sub-goals to be achieved to ensure your success

- adopted the quantum leap approach to set your sights high and to achieve demanding goals

- written down why you *believe* you will succeed in order to identify why your success goals are important to you, why they are achievable, what obstacles may have to be overcome and what priorities you need to focus on

- recognised the importance of achieving balance in your life by finding time to do things for your health and your relationships with family and friends

2 | HOW TO ASSESS YOUR TIME MANAGEMENT SKILLS

When you have read this chapter, *and implemented it*, you will:

- have assessed the potential for improving your *effective* time management
- recognise the specific ways in which you need to manage time more effectively
- use Pareto's Law – the 80/20 rule – to concentrate on the 20 per cent of your work which produces 80 per cent of the results
- have defined and ranked in order of importance the *key results* to be achieved in your job
- have identified and ranked the *major opportunites* to be realised in your job
- have assessed whether or not you allocate enough time to the key results and major opportunities

Time management skills are similar to 'getting on with people'; we all think we are pretty good at these things. So why not put your time management skills to the test by completing the following questionnaire.

Time management assessment

Do you:

1. Have success goals written down?

2. Agree your success goals with your boss wherever he or she should be involved?

3. Give the impression to people that you are well organised, really on top of your job, and still seem to have time for people?

4. Find enough time to tackle the important projects?

5. Have a reputation for invariably meeting deadlines?

6. Ask your secretary which jobs she could do for you?

7. Work away from the office occasionally to concentrate on a particular job?

8. Reply to correspondence quickly?

9. Regularly return telephone calls sufficiently promptly?

10. Make enough use of technology and office equipment to save you time?

11. Deliberately decide to leave certain jobs undone, until someone complains?

12. Make a list of what jobs and telephone calls must or should be done today?

13. Often take work home or go into the office at weekends?

14. Feel it is better to do a job yourself than to train someone else to do it for you?

15. Allow people to waste your time by dropping in for a chat?

16. Literally open the post each morning?

17. Write things in longhand for your secretary to type?

18. Spend time doing jobs which a junior person could do as well as you?

19. Arrange your own meetings?

20. Waste time filing things or finding files and information?

21. Sometimes go home feeling the day has been consumed by interruptions?

22. Accept telephone calls during informal meetings?

23. Spend too much time in unproductive meetings?

24. Arrive late for meetings quite often?

25. Spend too much time being chased by others and chasing others about missed deadlines?

26. Feel you are too much of a perfectionist for your own good?

27. Accept requests to do something, when it makes more sense for someone else to do it?

To score 100 per cent, you should have answered 'yes' to questions 1 to 12 and 'no' to questions 13 to 27.

If you scored 100 per cent, then you really do take time management seriously and you have already much of the success you want to achieve. If you scored between 21 and 26, then you manage your time effectively enough to know that you will achieve further improvement in your time management skills by reading and actioning the relevant chapters of this book. If you scored 20 or less, you should be determined to read and action this whole book systematically.

By now, however, you have already got a head start over most other people – because you have defined your success goals and really do believe you will achieve them.

There really is no substitute for writing down your success goals and the reasons why you will achieve them as described in Chapter 1. If you did omit this step, or simply said to yourself, 'I don't need to bother writing my success goals down on paper,' please do it now. Writing down your goals helps to reinforce them in your mind, and means that you can and should remind yourself of them by reading them again quite often. This alone will improve the likelihood of your achieving the success you want.

Assuming you did score less than 100 per cent in the questionnaire, there are some fundamental features of effective time management which need to be addressed at the outset.

Work is the biggest problem you face. Do remember and wholeheartedly adopt the slogan mentioned in the Preface, 'never confuse work and results'.

Work is often the enemy of achievement. Pareto's Law, referred to widely as the 80/20 rule, certainly applies to work. A useful way of expressing Pareto's Law is, '20 per cent often produces or accounts for 80 per cent'. For example:

20 per cent of the customers produce 80 per cent of total sales

20 per cent of products account for 80 per cent of profit

20 per cent of staff account for 80 per cent of absenteeism

and, especially,

20 per cent of the work you do often accounts for 80 per cent of the results your achieve

Sometimes it is worse still: 10 per cent of the work you do will produce 90 per cent of the results you want.

Sadly, some people are so 'busy' doing the work which comes their way that they simply don't have time to do the 20 per cent of work, or even 10 per cent, which they know deep down will produce 80 or 90 per cent of their results for them.

So key messages to consciously remember and act upon are: '*In any situation identify the key results to be achieved*,' and, '*Allocate plenty of time for the most important issues and opportunities*.' Once again, we all tend to think we adopt these approaches sufficiently well, and quite often we are fooling ourselves.

Consider the salesperson covering a sales territory. A typical approach is to 'plan the territory' so that the salesperson achieves:

- regular calls upon every customer
- more frequent calls upon customers who place orders more often

Never confuse work and results

- route planning to minimise the time wasted travelling between sales calls

- some time to call upon potential and former customers

This is an attempt at time management, but it cannot be described as allowing plenty of time for the most important sales opportunities. An effective time management approach may require spending a morning not making any sales visits and therefore not earning any commission. Instead, the morning should be used identifying and planning to pursue the main chances and important opportunities. You may be thinking, 'It is easy for him to say that, and of course he is right, but how do you actually do it?' Well, here goes.

Identify your five largest customers at present. Write down against the name of each one:

- the value of business they place with you

- the value of business they place with your competitors

- the amount of additional business you *believe* you can win

- why they buy from your competitors

Identify the five other customers with the largest amount of potential business you believe you could win, regardless of the value of business you do with them at present. Write down against the name of each one:

- the value of business they place with you

- the amount of additional business you *believe* you can win

- what you and your company need to do to achieve it

Identify the five most important non-customers in terms of the potential business you believe you could win. Write down against the name of each one:

- the amount of potential business you believe you can win

- how you will find out who to contact and ensure they will agree to meet you

- what else you, your manager and your company need to do to win the business

By now you have listed fifteen customers. The next step is to focus on a maximum of five of these. The aim must be to select those customers which you believe will produce the most additional business for you in return for the time and effort required to achieve it. If you feel you don't know enough about each of the fifteen companies to select a target list knowledgeably, then your next step is to find out more about them. Once you have selected your target list, then plan how to succeed with each customer. Now you really are attacking the most important sales opportunities.

You may be thinking, 'That was an easy example to illustrate; my job as the Financial Analysis Manager of a large subsidiary company surely defies the 20/80 rule.'

The answer is that it certainly will if you let it happen. An actual situation illustrates the point. A Financial Analysis Manager joined a subsidiary company and inherited the task of producing monthly financial reports for each division and department within the business. His team was so overloaded that virtually all they could do each month was to produce the figures, and start again. To produce the annual budgeting exercise as well as the monthly results required substantial amounts of overtime.

In some ways the time management *appeared* effective. Unfortunately, for time management *to be effective* it must focus on the key results to be achieved and benefits to be provided.

The vital 20 per cent of the work, which would have produced 80 per cent of the benefits to the company, was not being done at all. Nearly all of the managers did nothing as a result of receiving the monthly reports for the simple reason that what they needed was a concise narrative report drawing conclusions and suggesting measures which should be taken to improve future results. More importantly still, the divisional managers wanted someone to discuss their results with them and to do 'ad hoc' financial analyses to improve profits and cash flow.

Even when this was pointed out to the Financial Analysis Manager, his response was disappointing. He misinterpreted the comments as criticism rather than constructive help. It was an example of the '120/20 rule'. You may not have read about this rule, but you may be applying it unknowingly. The 120/20 rule means that someone does 120 per cent of the work expected of them, and produces only 20 per cent of the required results.

Many jobs in a large business are really internal service functions, for example actuaries, book-keepers, clerks, distribution managers, engineers: you could go on through virtually every other letter of the alphabet. To do an outstanding job means that you need to agree with your 'internal customers' the amount, standard and cost of the services to be provided. In other words, your *key results* must be agreed with them. This means that you must manage your time to have sufficient time to discuss the key results to be achieved with your internal customers and then meet them regularly enough to ensure that the results are being delivered consistently.

Begin to focus on the key results and major opportunities of your job now. Write them down in descending order of importance. Complete the following questionnaire. In the right-hand column, rank each item, according to the time you spend achieving it, from one to five.

If you find that the key result or major opportunity which you rank number one because it is the most important, but only rank it number five in terms of the time spent achieving it, then this is a glaring example of not allocating enough time to the important issues.

Key results and major opportunities assessment

The key results to be achieved in order of importance:

Time spent on
them, ranked
1 to 5

1. ☐

2. ☐

3. ☐

4. ☐

5. ☐

The major opportunities to be pursued in order of importance:

Time spent on
them, ranked
1 to 5

1. ☐

2. ☐

3. ☐

4. ☐

5. ☐

You may be saying to yourself, 'I have written down my key results, but there are simply no opportunities in my job – let alone major ones.' Nonsense. There are opportunities in every job. It just requires getting into the habit of consciously looking for them every day.

Here are some examples to get you thinking:

- A word processor would reduce the retyping of lengthy contracts to incorporate amendments and produce revised contracts more quickly

- Monthly accounts can be produced more quickly if they are circulated hand written and not typed at all

- Many thousands of pounds will be saved each year if we take the trouble to segregate our waste materials, rather than throwing everything into one bin

- There must be large savings to be made if we take energy management seriously

- Genetically engineered alternatives will enable us to produce some of our food ingredients more cheaply and help us to overcome a foreseeable worldwide scarcity of natural raw materials

- We will ask the one subsidiary of a multinational whom we do business with to provide us with an introduction to their sister companies in this country

- We can get a lot of free editorial coverage in the trade press if we make the effort

You may feel that some of the above examples are not *major* opportunities. An opportunity is only a major one relative to a particular job.

Opportunities are, by definition, things which do not *have* to be pursued. If you do spot a major one and pursue it, however, you may achieve a quantum leap in your key results.

How to assess your time management skills – action checklist

By now, you should:

- believe you need to and will improve your time management skills

- know specific areas in which you can improve your time management for maximum benefit

- have ranked the key results to be achieved

- have identified and ranked the major opportunities

- be determined to allocate enough time to the key results and major opportunities

3 | HOW TO MAKE YOUR APPEARANCE ACCELERATE SUCCESS

When you have read this chapter, *and implemented it*, you will:

● realise the subtle and real way in which your appearance works either for or against your success, and is rarely ever neutral

● invest time and money in your appearance, and never begrudgingly

● make your dress and appearance *today* reflect the success goals you are determined to achieve

● use your appearance to win subconscious acceptance by those above you, your colleagues, your staff and your customers

● make the appearance of your office contribute positively to your success goals

Your dress and appearance provide you with an opportunity to rehearse for success. This means imagining how you will feel, thinking how you will feel, and acting as if you have already achieved your success goals.

One of the most tangible ways to rehearse for success is to look the part today which you wish to play in the future. When you do this, people will begin 'seeing you' in the role that you wish to play. They may never mention it to you, they may not be aware of it consciously, but your appearance will be working for you. They will feel comfortable and at ease with you.

An interesting example of the effect of appearance is a highly success-ful lawyer who specialises in the popular music field. His clients include

Rehearse for success

some of the most successful recording artists, as well as up and coming groups anxious to negotiate their contracts shrewdly and not simply accept whatever terms and conditions are proposed by the record company.

In his own office, the lawyer looks just like someone from the pop music fraternity. He might be dressed in a sweatshirt, baggy trousers, leg warmers and trainers. Artists surely feel at ease with him. Whenever he is in court on behalf of a client, perhaps over a disputed contract, he is dressed in the way the judge finds acceptable – wearing the kind of suit and tie associated with a lawyer.

He has extended his image to his office surroundings. His office looks like the study of an outstandingly successful person in the music industry. On the walls are gold and platinum discs presented to him by his clients and photographs taken showing him relaxing with them.

In the office is a stereo sound system and a large collection of records and tapes. His clients must feel at home when they visit him. For a group still only dreaming about success, here is someone who demonstrably helps people to reach the top.

Don't dismiss the above example as an extreme case. Stop and think. Take stock of your dress, appearance and office. A good way to start is to observe carefully those people who have already achieved the success goals you have set for yourself, and preferably have progressed even further.

Consider an engineer who wishes to become a Technical Director of a subsidiary company in his group or a secretary determined to become a Media Executive in the advertising agency in which she works.

The first step is to look carefully at the dress and appearance of people who are Technical Directors or Media Executives. Then to do the same with the people they report to, and with the men and women at the top of the whole company. Successful dress and appearance require attention to detail every day. Obvious proof of this is when someone otherwise smart in appearance is let down by wearing a scruffy pair of shoes.

From your observation of people who are already successful, identify specific areas in which you will improve your dress and appearance in order to rehearse success. Do it systematically in the following way:

Hair   It is money well spent to visit a first-class hairdresser regularly. In a subtle but real way this will help you to feel good about yourself. If you don't know which hairdresser you should choose, why not ask someone whose hair always looks good?

Weight   If you are visibly overweight, this tends to work against you. So why not set yourself an achievable goal to lose some weight? By the way, medical advice seems to be to lose weight slowly and steadily, no more than about one kilo a week.

Clothes   A sound approach is to buy a basic wardrobe of good clothes and then to spend time to take care of them so they will last. Make sure that the colours you wear co-ordinate well together. Men are much more likely to wear stockings which clash with the rest of their clothes than women.

Accessories   A careful choice of accessories can add style to your appearance without becoming too exaggerated. Belts, ties and jewellery fall into this category, and so do wristwatches, pens and briefcases. Choose accessories to create and reflect the image you want. The smartest clothes will be let down if you pull out a cheap plastic ball pen and carry a battered briefcase.

To ensure you do improve your dress and appearance, complete the following questionnaire. Give yourself marks out of ten for each item, using the benchmark that a rating of ten out of ten represents an asset which will positively help you to achieve your success goals.

Dress and appearance improvement

Score out of 10

Hair ☐
Action to be taken:

Amount to be invested:

Target date:

Weight ☐
Target weight:

Target date:

Clothes ☐
Action to be taken:

Amount to be invested:

Target date:

Accessories ☐
Action to be taken:

Amount to be invested:

Target date:

Shoes ☐
Action to be taken:

Amount to be invested:

Target date:

Total amount to be invested £........   Score out of 50   ☐

Dress and appearance are so important to help you achieve your success goals that filling in a questionnaire is not enough. Make an entry in your diary *now*, to remind you in three months' time to recalculate your score out of 50, and to add to the list of actions you will take.

Your office

Decide now that when you arrive at work tomorrow morning you will take stock of your office.

This is how to do it. As you walk into your office, stop in the doorway, stand there and consciously assess the overall impression it gives. Does it already reflect the success goals you are to achieve? Are you sure? Have you examined the offices of people who have already achieved what you want?

Most people are allocated an office, and have no choice in the matter. If you own the business, or are the managing director, or even the branch manager, then you may be able to choose the size of your office. Either way, your office speaks volumes about you – for better or worse. Some examples will make the point, each one of them accurate in every detail.

The solicitor in private practice   Her desk is littered with files. The in-tray is overflowing. There are about a dozen telephone messages scattered on the desk, presumably unanswered. A side table is over-loaded with files. More files are simply kept in piles on the floor, and on a couple of chairs as well.

This office says to clients: this solicitor is so disorganised and over-loaded that you are unlikely to get the priority and attention you deserve.

The owner of a successful insurance broking company   His office is excessively large and extravagantly furnished. On the walls are a photo-graph of his luxury yacht moored permanently in Marbella, another one of his impressive villa in the Algarve, and an oil painting of one of his racehorses. In contrast, his staff work in cramped conditions.

This office says to his staff, who are not particularly well paid: the owner is using us to make him even richer and to spend his time enjoying himself whilst we attend to the business for him.

The chief executive of a small public company   His office occupies the top floor of a costly office block in a major city. He does not have a desk, but sits at a large dining table. There are three settees, a large drinks cabinet, a television set and video recorder. There are no obvious signs of work such as a filing cabinet, a bookcase or papers being worked on.

This office says to professional advisers who visit him and his board colleagues: not a lot of work goes on in here.

The impressions the offices described above give about their occupants may be inaccurate, but unfortunately visitors are likely to believe them.

You may be thinking to yourself, 'These are extreme examples. My office is not as bad as that.' Nonetheless, there are things which can and should be done about your office.

Walls and ceiling   You simply do not have to accept a dirty or shabby appearance. If the company are not prepared to repaint your office, request approval to do it yourself during a weekend.

Tidiness   Tidiness is an aspect of effective time management. A tidy desk and office conveys an air of efficiency and contributes to your efficiency. Things are less likely to get 'lost' or overlooked, and less time will be wasted in finding what you need. There is simply no excuse for an untidy office. A good discipline is to leave a completely clear desk top and tidy office every evening.

Things on the walls   Once again, these are likely to create a positive or negative impression rather than a neutral one. Start by eliminating the negative. Any picture or cartoon with the least sexual connotation should be removed immediately. At worst it may offend people of both sexes, at best it may be regarded as a sign of your immaturity.

Notices pinned on the wall look untidy, are often out of date and irrelevant. Take them all down, and keep any which you need to refer to handy in an indexed ring binder or suchlike.

Then accentuate the positive. Put up things on the wall which focus on achievement. These could include:

- a framed copy of an award
- photographs of projects completed or exhibition stands
- graphs showing the progress to date towards the achievement of key results

Your aim should be to have a minimum number, each one well presented, to have the maximum impact.

Add your personal style

People often inherit a picture or two along with an office. Many office pictures are awful. Pot plants which are past their best or dying from a lack of regular watering don't help either. So throw them out.

Ask your manager, if you need to ask, for approval to spend a modest amount on pictures and plants. If your request is refused, then spend your own money on things which reflect you, your good taste, your own style and your success to date. Treat yourself, you will have the enjoyment of them and you can take them with you when you go. A modest amount spent on a couple of limited edition prints, a striking plant in an attractive ceramic pot, and perhaps a small piece of sculpture will transform your office.

To make sure you do improve the appearance of your office, complete the following questionnaire. Give yourself marks out of ten for each item, a score of ten indicating that you have already achieved a standard in keeping with your success goals.

Office improvement

Wall and ceiling decoration
Action to be taken:

Tidiness
Action to be taken:

Things on the walls
Action to be taken:

Adding your personal style
Action to be taken:

Total score out of 40:

Make an entry in your diary *now*, to remind you a month from today to recalculate your score out of 40 and to check that the action has been completed.

How to make your appearance accelerate success – action checklist

By now, you will:

- be committed to an action plan to make your dress and appearance *already reflect* the achievement of your success goals

- have decided how to make your office already reflect your success goals

- have begun to *rehearse for success*; imagining, thinking and acting *now* as if you had already achieved your success goals

- have made diary entries to ensure you do achieve the improvement you want to make in your dress, appearance and office

4 | HOW TO MANAGE YOUR MANAGER

When you have read this chapter, *and implemented it*, you will have:

- agreed with your manager the key results, standards of performance, and deadlines to be achieved, which he or she regards as *outstanding achievement*

- found out to what degree your manager feels you are already delivering outstanding achievement

- got on your manager's wavelength by understanding the priorities, pressures and constraints he or she faces and the outstanding achievement he or she is committed to deliver

- negotiated the resources and support needed for you to produce outstanding achievement

- agreed the *major opportunities* to be pursued

- gained your manager's positive help and commitment to ensure you produce outstanding achievement

You may be thinking, 'When are we going to concentrate purely on time management in this book.' Well, you aren't going to be allowed to fall into that trap.

My first job after leaving university was as a management trainee. At the end of two weeks' initial training, each trainee was given a specific job as promised during the selection interviews. We met the chairman who told us to regard this job as the most important one we would ever have. My face dropped visibly, until he pointed out that unless we did our first job well enough we would not get another one in the company.

Even if your success goal is to achieve rapid promotion, producing outstanding achievement in your present job can only help you. Your immediate manager, not you, is the most important judge of what constitutes outstanding achievement in your present job. So it is vital that you and your manager overtly agree what constitutes outstanding achievement. To assume you are in agreement can be downright dangerous.

Until you have got this agreement, what you believe is effective time management may be misdirected. This means that an essential part of time management is to agree with your immediate manager what he regards to be outstanding achievement in terms of:

- key results to be produced

- standards of performance to be maintained

- priorities to be chosen and deadlines to be met

Before you discuss this with your immediate manager for the first time, do your homework, especially if you have only recently joined your company or subsidiary. Be ready to propose what you regard as outstanding achievement. Wherever possible suggest measurable results, standards, priorities and deadlines to minimise the scope for disagreement about your achievement. Make sure that you do not propose unnecessarily high standards. The yardstick should be fitness for the purpose, at an acceptable cost.

Complete the key results statement which follows so that you have got clearly thought out ideas to discuss with your manager.

Key results statement

Listed in order of importance:

1. Key result

   Standard of performance

   Priority/deadline

2. Key result

   Standard of performance

   Priority/deadline

3. Key result

   Standard of performance

   Priority/deadline

4. Key result

   Standard of performance

   Priority/deadline

5. Key result

   Standard of performance

   Priority/deadline

Understand the constraints and pressures on your manager

The members of an effective management team need to be on the same wavelength. They must be in agreement about the key results and standards to be achieved, and the broad philosophy and policies to be applied. They must also have an understanding of pressures, constraints, and individual strengths and weaknesses.

To produce results which your manager will regard as outstanding achievement, it is helpful to know what results are expected of him or her, and the pressures and constraints he or she faces. With this knowledge, you should feel confident that you really are pulling together in the same direction.

Ask for an appraisal of your performance

Management appraisal schemes are a good idea, and often mismanaged awfully in practice. Managers need to be trained to carry out formal management appraisal interviews. Staff often feel that the appraisal interview is merely used to justify the level of salary increase, amount of bonus awarded, or failure to receive a promotion.

Regardless of whether or not your company operates a management appraisal scheme, set up one with your manager on your terms.

It is both reasonable and commendable that having agreed with your manager what constitutes outstanding achievement, you should ask for his objective assessment of how your present performance matches up. You are asking for critical comment and not asking for a salary increase.

Some managers find it difficult to tell people of shortcomings in performance but find no difficulty in telling their own manager about your shortcomings. You may find that your manager does not view your achievement anything like as highly as you do. Whilst this may come as a shock, the sooner you know the better it is. What is more, it happens more frequently than you might think because people do not communicate openly with each other.

Negotiate the resources to ensure success

There are no prizes awarded, and rightly so, to someone who performs tolerably well despite making do with inadequate resources or support. The only acceptable time to negotiate the resources and support needed is when you agree with your immediate manager the outstanding achievement to be produced. If you need more staff or more cash, be ready to outline exactly what you need and the tangible benefits which will be produced.

Be prepared for being told that no more resources are available. Be ready to suggest ways in which you could revise your targets for outstanding achievement to be compatible with the resources available, but make sure you do it in a positive way.

If you meet with a King Canute-like approach from your manager, namely that you are expected to produce results with inadequate resources, then *you must negotiate now*. Put him on the spot by seeking his advice. Ask him how he suggests you should produce the results he regards as outstanding achievement with the resources available to you.

Obtain the support needed for outstanding achievement

When you have negotiated to have sufficient staff of the appropriate calibre in your department, you are still likely to need considerable help and support from other departments or suppliers to enable you to produce outstanding achievement.

For example, you may need to have a piece of software written by a specialist department within the company, only to find yourself nearly at the end of the queue as far as they are concerned.

Identify and list the obstacles standing in the way of outstanding achievement. It is worth listing external and internal obstacles separately. If you are a production manager, an external obstacle may be that a specialist sub-contractor is failing to meet the standards of quality and speed of delivery you require. An internal obstacle may be that you do not receive an analysis of your 'reject costs' to enable you to reduce them. It is quite unacceptable to complain about obstacles like these and not to overcome them. Surprisingly, people are more likely to accept internal obstacles as an inevitable hazard of corporate life, rather than external ones. It is really a case of shooting yourself in the foot and then complaining of the pain, if you allow this to happen.

Write down the external and internal obstacles which confront you. Against each one specify the action needed to overcome it, and any help needed from other people.

External obstacles to be overcome

In order of importance:

1. Obstacle

   Action to be taken:

   Help needed from:

2. Obstacle

   Action to be taken:

   Help needed from:

3. Obstacle

   Action to be taken:

   Help needed from:

4. Obstacle

   Action to be taken:

   Help needed from:

5. Obstacle

   Action to be taken:

   Help needed from:

Internal obstacles to be overcome

In order of importance:

1. Obstacle

    Action to be taken:

    Help needed from:

2. Obstacle

    Action to be taken:

    Help needed from:

3. Obstacle

    Action to be taken:

    Help needed from:

4. Obstacle

    Action to be taken:

    Help needed from:

5. Obstacle

    Action to be taken:

    Help needed from:

Agree the major opportunities to pursue

Outstanding achievement requires more than doing your job as it exists today. You need to identify and evaluate major opportunities to be pursued. Once again, the word 'major' applies in relation to the demands of your job.

Pursuing major opportunities may be summed up as going for the main chance in your present job. It needs imagination, so some examples will be given for people doing different kinds of jobs.

Chief Executive of a public company   To pursue a major opportunity to take over a much larger company in the same industry, because it is not doing well at present, in order to become the market leader.

Managing Director of a subsidiary engineering company   To find attractive private companies operating in niche markets to acquire.

'But,' I hear you saying, 'looking for acquisitions is done by group staff, and I am not sure they would regard it as part of my job.' Nonsense, if it is a major opportunity for you, *make it* part of your job. If you need some help to do it, why not ask group staff to second someone temporarily to you?

Marketing Director   To accelerate nationwide coverage by franchising the operation in selected territories.

Manufacturing Director   To evaluate the benefits which may be gained from automated warehousing and 'just-in-time' inventory management even though no one has used these techniques in your industry on a major scale as far as you know.

Furniture Buyer   To look for exciting merchandise from countries such as South Korea.

To produce outstanding achievement you need to be a self-starter, and to develop the habit of continuously and consciously looking for major

. . . Consciously looking for major opportunities

opportunities. Do not confuse 'bright ideas' with major opportunities. A bright idea is often no more than an ill-thought-out and half-baked scheme. A bright idea needs to be carefully evaluated for it to become a major opportunity.

Turn a bright idea into a major opportunity by writing down for each proposal:

- the purpose and results to be achieved

- other *tangible benefits* to be produced

- the method to be adopted

- the cost and timescale involved

- the financial return to be achieved

There is no substitute for clear and rigorous thinking; and writing your ideas down helps. You will quickly see whether or not the proposal really is a major opportunity. If not, throw it out.

People often confuse the proposal and the purpose. A proposal may be to buy a personal computer. The purpose to be achieved may be to overcome the situation whereby the present electromechanical machine is overloaded and to provide for the future needs of a growing business. The proposal is only one means of achieving the purpose. Before you 'fall in love' with your own bright idea, list as many different proposals as you can identify.

Do your preparation thoroughly before presenting major opportunities to your manager. For each one, complete a major opportunity proposal as outlined here. Do remember as well, however, to ask your manager what major opportunities he feels you should be pursuing.

Major opportunity proposal

Purpose and results to be achieved:

Proposal:

Other tangible benefits to be produced:

Methods to be adopted:

Costs and timescale:

Financial return to be achieved:

Win positive help and commitment

It is only enlightened self-interest for a manager to want his staff to succeed. What is more, most managers welcome the opportunity to help their staff.

So *involve your manager*, win his positive help and commitment to your achieving your goals. Identify specific ways in which your manager, and if necessary his manager as well, can help you succeed. Possible help could include:

- sharing some of his technical expertise with you

- arranging a specific training course for you

- providing a personal introduction to someone

- working with you on a particularly complex task

Ask to be told immediately whenever your manager feels you are falling short of outstanding achievement. The worst thing you can allow to happen to you is only to find out about your shortcomings at an annual appraisal interview.

How to manage your manager – action checklist

By now, you will have:

- written and agreed a key results statement

- had your achievement appraised, *at your request*

- understand the priorities, pressures and constraints on your manager

- negotiated the resources you need for outstanding achievement

- listed the external and internal obstacles to success and written down how you will overcome them

- identified, developed and evaluated major opportunity proposals

- obtained positive help and commitment from your manager

5 | HOW TO CREATE AND LEAD A WINNING TEAM

When you have read this chapter, *and implemented it*, you will:

- lead by personal example

- have recruited staff of the calibre needed to produce outstanding achievement

- create and maintain excitement throughout your team

- give people freedom by effective delegation

- invest your time to train and to develop your team

- be willing to promote people outside your department when appropriate

- create 'free time' for yourself to produce even more outstanding achievement

Before the chapter has begun, you are probably saying to yourself, 'If only it was that easy.' Well, it is that easy! More importantly, too, in the previous chapters you have already laid sound foundations.

There are countless books written about managerial leadership. The approach described here may be regarded as old-fashioned, even unfashionable, but it has the advantage that it is tried and tested – and will succeed for you.

Lead by personal example

Personal example is a powerful force which provides a firm basis for effective leadership. Take heart from the ways you have improved the personal example you set for your team by having worked through some of this book already.

Let's remind you of what you should have achieved already. You have:

- defined your success goals in writing and you believe you *will* achieve them

- adopted the quantum leap approach to ensure your success goals are sufficiently demanding

- identified the key results to be achieved and major opportunities to be pursued

- made plans to ensure your dress, appearance and office *already* reflect the achievement of your success goals

- written down a key results statement for outstanding achievement

- identified and evaluated major opportunity proposals

- identified obstacles in the way of outstanding achievement and made plans to overcome them

Recruit people to achieve outstanding success

A key element of time management is recruiting a team of the calibre needed to achieve outstanding success. This does not suggest that you should recruit a team of potential chief executives, unless for some exceptional reason this is exactly what you do need. People who are over-qualified or over-talented for a position are likely to become bored with it quite quickly, and their performance is likely to fall short of their ability.

If a manager complains about the quality of staff when he or she has been in charge long enough to change or develop them, it is more likely that the problem is being caused by either the manager or the company, and not by the staff. If the company refuses to allow the manager to replace or transfer people or to encourage them to leave, then the manager should question whether or not the company really wants outstanding achievement and be prepared to leave. If the manager has the authority to replace people, and doesn't have the courage to do it, then the shortcomings rest with him or her.

Unless you recruit sufficient people of the appropriate calibre, it doesn't matter how effective your personal time management is, you may well:

- end up working the hours expected of a workaholic
- never see the situation improve
- fail to deliver outstanding achievement

Choose to be a resultaholic, not a workaholic. Resultaholics achieve more with less personal time and effort. Workaholics enjoy work, and often confuse it with results.

Create and maintain excitement

True leaders exude excitement! Their enthusiasm is contagious. They are not deterred by setbacks.

'But,' you are saying to yourself, 'I am just not like that, it doesn't come easily to me.' Hold on, don't put yourself down so mistakenly. Aren't you excited by the key results you have set for yourself? Don't you believe enthusiastically that you and your team will achieve them? That you will not be deterred by setbacks, because you have already identified major obstacles and how you will overcome them?

Now you need to be a salesperson, and to sell your key results to your team. Again, do your homework first and *rehearse for success*. Consider

True leaders exude excitement!

whether you should see the senior members of your team individually or together. Sell them, not tell them, the key results. Make sure you give them a sense of involvement. Then consider having a meeting of your whole department to sell them the key results. Make it a dialogue not a monologue. Ask people:

- do you want to achieve the key results?

- do you believe we can and will achieve them?

- what will make your job more interesting and enjoyable?

- what clash of priorities, shortage of resources, obstacles and constraints do we need to overcome?

- what ideas do you have to overcome them?

- what major opportunities should we pursue?

Remember, the best ideas do not necessarily come with seniority. What's more, achievement and success help to create excitement and to motivate people. So set up regular meetings to keep people informed of progress against key results, and to keep listening to their problems and the solutions they recommend.

Some managers use competitions to create and maintain excitement, and achieve this with quite modest prizes. You should design competitions which create as many winners as possible.

Consider a chain of estate agent's offices. If expensive prizes are to be given to, say, the top three salespersons during the year, then the consequences may be:

- many of the salespeople will know they are extremely unlikely to win one of the three prizes from the outset

- as soon as a handful of salespeople achieve a commanding lead, most of the others will stop any special effort they have been making

- the sales support staff are likely to feel that they are never given the chance to win a prize

An alternative approach, designed to produce as many winners as possible, may be to offer modest prizes to be won:

- every month

- by every person

- in every office

- which exceeds their monthly target

The prizes should be different each month to maintain interest and excitement. A prize of a bottle of pink champagne may be exciting one month, but it would become boring if offered month after month.

There are other simple and inexpensive ways to add interest and excitement. People who work in an office five days a week and have little opportunity to see the products or service for themselves are likely to welcome the opportunity to visit:

- the company stand at an exhibition or trade show

- an installation or branch

- a sports or cultural event sponsored by the company

It is not enough just to agree that a manager should help to make work exciting. Complete the excitement action list which follows *now*.

Excitement action list

Specific action to be taken to create and maintain excitement:

1. Action:

   Target date:

2. Action:

   Target date:

3. Action:

   Target date:

4. Action:

   Target date:

5. Action:

   Target date:

Select what to delegate

Are you caught in a time management trap? There is a simple test to find out. Do you feel that you are overworked because none of your staff are able to do certain jobs properly, so you have to do them? If this is the situation, you have either created it or allowed it continue. The good news is that you can and will overcome it.

Most managers spend a significant amount of time doing work which one of their staff has the capability to do as well, or even better. Develop the habit of giving away routine work. Reserve your time for what you need to do to deliver outstanding achievement.

Identify five time-consuming and routine tasks which you do regularly, or major annual jobs which you do yourself. Write down for each one:

- which member of your team could do this job

- what *exactly* is stopping you giving the task away

- what you will do to give the task away effectively

'But,' I hear you saying, 'I am not guilty on this score, I am genuinely overworked because I am so valuable to the company.' If you think this, try a simple test. Ask senior members of your team what jobs they would like to take over from you. It may come as a surprise to you, but almost invariably this will produce suggestions of tasks which you should not be doing yourself.

Owners of businesses tend to be worse offenders than managers. An example illustrates just what can happen. A man in his fifties had built up a sizeable business importing kitchenware items, which were sold to retailers. No other members of his family wished to work in the business. He found himself a wealthy man, unable to enjoy his wealth because he found he 'had' to work about eighty hours each week. He was convinced that the answer was to upgrade his computer systems, but was eventually persuaded to choose effective time management instead.

It soon became clear that most of his time was spent supervising the sales office and organising despatch to customers. The reasons were that his sales office team were not sufficiently familiar with the large product range to answer telephone enquiries and that he was keen to route plan each delivery truck every day to minimise the cost of distribution. The solution was obvious to someone else, and inexpensive for him. An experienced manager was recruited to manage the sales office and despatch, with a specific brief to give the sales office team the detailed product knowledge needed to handle queries themselves.

Unfortunately, the business problem was worse than this. The overworked owner had not met a single customer for over a year. He had 'delegated' this to two salespeople, but a more accurate word was he had *abdicated* a key task. Analysis showed that eight customers, out of a total of over five hundred, accounted for about 60 per cent of total sales in the previous financial year. Of these eight customers, during the current year one had stopped trading with the company and two had reduced their level of orders significantly. Yet the owner was 'too busy' to visit these customers himself.

Identify three key tasks which you are not doing at all, or are not spending enough time on. Remember, a key task is one which contributes significantly to the achievement of a key result, and which does require and justify your handling the task personally. Write down for each one:

- the results you can achieve by doing it yourself
- the amount of time required to do it adequately

Complete the work disposal and key tasks action lists which follow. Make sure that the total time you will save by giving work away because you should not be doing it personally comfortably exceeds the amount of extra time you plan to spend on key tasks to produce outstanding achievements.

Work disposal action list

Tasks to be given away to other team members:

Time to be saved:

1. Task:

    To be given to:
    Action needed:

    Target date:

2. Task:

    To be given to:
    Action needed:

    Target date:

3. Task:

    To be given to:
    Action needed:

    Target date:

4. Task:

    To be given to:
    Action needed:

    Target date:

5. Task:

    To be given to:
    Action needed:

    Target date:

Key task action list

Extra time to be invested on key tasks:

Time to be
invested:

1. Task:

   Action to be taken:

   Target date:

2. Task:

   Action to be taken:

   Target date:

3. Task:

   Action to be taken:

   Target date:

Delegate effectively

Nearly everyone will agree that successful delegation is a cornerstone of effective time management. Most of us feel quite sure that delegation is such a basic skill we have nothing to learn or improve in this area. Even if you feel this way, read this section merely as a checklist.

Effective delegation involves every one of the following steps:

Step 1 Agree the results and standards to be achieved

Note the use of the word *agree* rather than *define*. It is not good enough to *tell* people what you expect. Obtain agreement, and better still, encourage the person to recommend the results and standards to be achieved. Effective delegation begins with positive commitment, and mere acquiescence is totally unacceptable. Make sure the results and standards are defined clearly, and don't rely on the assumption that you both know instinctively what is required.

Step 2 Agree the completion date

The preferred way is for the person to recommend their own deadline. If you set it, make sure the person feels that they have the resources and support to achieve the deadline without other things suffering.

Step 3 Agree interim checkpoints

Agree dates when interim milestones of progress will have been reached. Put the onus on the other person to let you know that each checkpoint has been reached on time. Otherwise you will waste your time and cause justifiable irritation by unnecessarily checking up on people too often.

Step 4 Explain the importance, the context and the constraints

Make sure the person understands the overall picture, and this applies especially to the newer members of your team. Otherwise you are likely to find yourself saying, 'I never thought you would have done it in that way.'

Step 5 Provide the authority required

Make sure the person has the authority to obtain information, to make visits, to contact people, and to spend within a budgeted amount, in order to avoid wasting your time in giving specific approval on every occasion. Equally, make sure that the other people affected know of the authority given, otherwise you will waste time receiving phone calls which begin, 'Is it OK for . . .'

Step 6 Police the agreed deadlines

Do not create false priorities. Show your dissatisfaction if you have not been informed that checkpoints have not been reached on time or deadlines not met. If you need to change priorities for someone, be ready to amend deadlines rather than let some slip. Create an environment in which deadlines are met consistently.

Step 7 Say thank you

How often have you heard people say to you, 'My boss never even said thank you to me and I really put myself out for him.' Of course, people think that about their manager, but tell other people. There is no excuse for omitting to say 'thank you' *every time*. If you feel that you are too busy to say thank you, then you have a serious time management problem.

People are delighted to receive the words 'thank you'. The achievement may be sufficient to merit a written note of thanks as well, with a copy sent to your own manager. Small gifts work wonders. If someone worked until midnight last evening *for you*, give them some flowers or a bottle of wine the next day.

Invest time to train and develop your team

The investment of time to train and develop people is another cornerstone of effective time management. You cannot afford not to do it. If you train someone once to do a job countless times instead of you, the payoff is enormous.

Development goes an important step further. It equips people to take on more responsibility, to become more valuable to the company, and to achieve their personal goals without leaving. Investing time to develop people is another example of enlightened self-interest. You know the disruption caused when a competent person chooses to leave. *You* have to spend time recruiting a replacement and much time has to be spent introducing someone into a company and allowing them to gain the local knowledge required. In the meantime, achievement will be reduced and the workload inevitably increased.

'But,' I hear you saying, 'I agree with you, but what should I actually do about it?'

Sit down with each person reporting directly to you and discuss:

- their own success goals
- training which would be helpful
- ways to make their job more rewarding and enjoyable
- their next job within the company

To develop a kindred spirit, which helps to create a coherent team, perhaps you should suggest that your staff obtain a copy of this book and work through it for themselves. Certainly encourage them to have a similar discussion with each person reporting directly to them.

Training and development are so important that you should complete the personal training and development programme that follows for each person reporting to you, *and yourself*.

Personal training and development programme

Person ....Year ....

Training to be completed:

Personal development to be completed:

Promote people unselfishly

You cannot reasonably expect people to be committed to helping you to produce outstanding achievement so you can realise your success goals and not to gain timely promotion as a reward.

If you cannot promote someone sufficiently soon within your own department, help them to be promoted elsewhere within the company. 'But,' I hear you saying, 'isn't this against my interests?' Definitely not, because the benefits to you include:

- the person being promoted will want to ensure a smooth handover and to install their replacement effectively

- you may have an opportunity to make internal promotions as a result of the vacancy or to reorganise the team more effectively

- your reputation for developing and promoting people unselfishly is enhanced, which encourages other outstanding people to want to join your team

- both the person promoted and new manager will feel you have done them a favour, and either of them may become your boss one day

Create free time for yourself

Gradually, as you create a winning team, you will find that you have free time, which will enable you to invest it to identify and pursue the major opportunities which will produce a further quantum leap in your achievements.

How to create and lead a winning team – action checklist

By now, you will have:

- identified the recruitment you need to make to ensure outstanding achievement

- written an action plan to create and maintain excitement amongst your team

- created action lists to give away routine work and to focus on the key tasks you need to handle for outstanding achievement

- checked that you really do delegate effectively

- made a habit of saying thank you every time for a job well done

- written a personal training and development plan for each person reporting to you, *and for yourself*

- decided to promote people unselfishly

- found that already your own free time is increasing

6 | HOW TO UTILISE YOUR SECRETARY AS A PERSONAL ASSISTANT

When you have read this chapter, *and implemented it*, you will:

- manage your time more effectively by using your secretary as a personal assistant

- regard her as a vital member of your team

- allow her to be more productive by wasting less of her time

- have given work away to her

- have discussed training and career development opportunities with her

- keep her better informed of the overall picture to enable her to be on the same wavelength as you

'But,' you may be saying to yourself, 'What difference does a job title make, and anyway my boss may feel I have got delusions of seniority if I suggested it.'

Effective time management requires that *you change the role of your secretary* so she becomes a valuable personal assistant. Whether you change her job title is a separate matter and entirely up to you. If your team consists of just you and your secretary, then she is especially valuable.

Most managers fail to make effective use of their secretaries. Put yourself to the test *now*. Complete the assessment which follows to reveal your effective use of your personal assistant. Use it to write down the jobs she does in addition to typing and receiving incoming telephone calls.

You change the role of your secretary

Effective use of your personal assistant

Tasks handled for me:

1.

2.

3.

4.

5.

Tasks which should be handled for me:

1.

2.

3.

4.

5.

Tasks which should not be done at all:

1.

2.

3.

4.

5.

Things which waste her time:

1.

2.

3.

4.

5.

'But,' I hear you saying to yourself, 'this is the only difficult questionnaire in the book.' So here are some ideas to get you thinking:

Jobs your personal assistant has the capability to handle for you

- arranging meetings
- all filing
- writing, not just typing, routine letters and replies
- deciding which mail you will wish to see and then give to someone else to action, distributing mail which you do not even need to see, and sorting the remainder into categories:

  – mail requiring your attention urgently
  – 'you should decide who should deal with it'
- making telephone calls for you which are simply giving information or confirming arrangements
- asking the caller for the purpose of their call in an attempt to action it for you, whether you are available or not
- operating a follow-up file to remind you when follow-up action is needed
- doing the follow-up for you whenever possible
- obtaining and collating information for you
- compiling routine weekly and monthly reports

Jobs your personal assistant should not be doing at all

- retyping whole pages because she does not use a word processor

- making coffee and tea for the whole department

- typing replies to internal memos, when a hand-written comment by you on the original is adequate

- unnecessarily typing urgent internal financial reports, when hand-written figures are sufficiently legible

Jobs which waste your personal assistant's time

- finding telephone numbers repeatedly for you instead of maintaining your own index for you

- struggling to read your hand-written manuscript drafts when you could use a dictating machine

- continually interrupting her work because you don't plan yours

Whatever the number of items you have entered in your questionnaire on your effective use of your personal assistant, do ask your personal assistant to answer the questionnaire as well. You are almost certain to get some good ideas you have not considered.

The next step is to turn your assessment into tangible results. Complete the personal action list which follows, *after discussion with her*.

Personal assistant action list

Jobs to be taken over from me:

1. Job:

   Target date:

2. Job:

   Target date:

3. Job:

   Target date:

4. Job:

   Target date:

5. Job:

   Target date:

Time-wasting

1. Cause:

   Person to take action:

2. Cause:

   Person to take action:

3. Cause:

   Person to take action:

4. Cause:

   Person to take action:

5. Cause:

   Person to take action:

Realise that you may be the person who wastes most of her time, albeit unwittingly. Ensure you do achieve effective time management by making a diary entry one month from today, to check that the personal assistant action list has been implemented.

Discuss training and development with your personal assistant

The education and intelligence of many secretaries compares favourably with their managers'. So progress towards a personal assistant role should be regarded as merely a first step in her career development. Discuss with your personal assistant:

- her career goals
- specific training she would like to have
- opportunities for personal development and career progress

Remember, many outstanding women executives started their working life as secretaries. So make sure you recognise and help to develop managerial potential wherever it exists.

Keep her informed of the overall picture

'But,' I hear you saying, 'shouldn't I be using my time effectively.' Yes, and you will benefit by spending a little time on giving your personal assistant an insight into the company position, your own goals, priorities, pressures, constraints and concerns. As a result, she will be able to help you to manage time effectively by, where appropriate:

- suggesting to someone requesting a meeting with you that a phone call will save you both time

81

- persuading people to visit you to avoid travelling time

- suggesting breakfast instead of lunch meetings to save time

- knowing when you should be interrupted, contacted during a visit, or telephoned at home because of the need for urgent action

- hold the fort adequately when you are out of the office

How to utilise your secretary as a personal assistant – action checklist

By now, you will have:

- recognised the need for your secretary to become your personal assistant in order to manage your time effectively

- helped your secretary to become a valuable personal assistant

- produced and agreed a personal assistant action list to give some of your work away and to avoid wasting her time

- discussed career goals and training, personal development and promotion opportunities with your personal assistant

- invested time to make your personal assistant aware of the wider picture to enable her to be of more help in your own effective time management

7 | HOW TO HOLD PRODUCTIVE MEETINGS

When you have read this chapter, *and implemented it*, you will:

- have assessed your meetings for effectiveness

- hold more productive and shorter meetings

- begin and finish meetings on time

- manage time during meetings to complete the agenda

- produce concise minutes for action and distribute them promptly

Meetings are essential, and meetings waste a large amount of management time. Both of these statements are true.

Meetings consume time in preparation and minute-writing, as well as attendance. Some managers mortgage up to 50 per cent of their working time by taking part in regular meetings. Quite often monthly performance review meetings are spent largely discussing the results for the previous month, *which are history*. You can analyse and discuss actual results, *but you can't change history*.

'But,' I hear you saying to yourself, 'how do I get off the treadmill I'm on?'

Value-analyse your formal meetings

For each of the meetings you hold regularly, read the minutes of the three most recent meetings and use a fluorescent highlighter pen to pick out the action agreed. Then answer these questions:

Effective meeting checklist

- Was the action agreed worth the time spent in preparation, attendance and minute writing?

- Was the total amount of time spent by those attending justified by the action agreed?

- Why should the meetings continue to be held?

- Why do you need to attend the meetings? Why not delegate the job to someone else and attend only when the situation or agenda merits your contribution?

- Why not hold them quarterly instead of monthly, or monthly instead of weekly, or only when either the actual results to date or the year-end forecast is more than 5 per cent below budget?

- Who needs to attend regularly? Who should be invited to attend when relevant? Who only needs to receive the minutes for information?

- Do you compile or authorise the agenda?

- Are the agenda and background papers circulated soon enough for people to come adequately prepared?

- Do the meetings start on time with everyone present?

- Do you check at the start of the meeting that the actions agreed at the previous meeting have been completed?

- How long do the meetings last? How long should they be allowed to last?

- Do you manage to complete the agenda within the scheduled time regularly?

- Do people know when the meetings are scheduled to finish? Do they finish on time?

- Is personal accountability and a deadline assigned to each item for action?

- Why are the minutes not restricted to a list of actions agreed?

- How soon after the meeting are the minutes circulated? Why aren't they circulated within twenty-four hours?

- How long do you spend either writing the minutes or approving them?

- What percentage of items are actioned by the due date?

- Why do you tolerate less than virtually 100 per cent?

- Have you asked those attending the above questions?

If you feel there is scope to manage the time concerned more effectively in regular meetings you hold, then you should:

- circulate a copy of the effective meeting checklist to those people attending along with the agenda

- include as the first item on the agenda 'meeting effectiveness assessment'

- ask people to read this chapter before the meeting

- ask them to come prepared with *specific recommendations* they wish to make

- make the final item of the agenda 'review of this meeting' to assess the meeting whilst it is still fresh in the minds of people.

'But,' I hear you saying to yourself, 'most of my time is spent attending meetings rather than holding them.' From now on be wholly positive. Say to yourself, 'And, what's more, I intend to do something about the meeting I attend as well as those I hold.'

So, take positive action. Decide the particular approach which will bring the most constructive response from the person who holds each regular meeting you attend. Possible approaches include:

- making specific recommendations to make the meetings more effective

- suggesting that a review of the meetings is put on the agenda of the next meeting

- inviting the person who holds the meeting to read this chapter

Value-analyse your informal meetings

These are the meetings involving one or two other people, and consume your time and often interrupt a key task you are working on. Answer the following questions about informal meetings you have.

Effective informal meeting checklist

- Do you always telephone to find out when it will be convenient for the other person to meet?

- When you telephone, do you briefly mention your purpose and agenda so that he will be prepared and indicate how long a discussion is needed? Do you ask if there is anything else he or she wishes to discuss to ensure you are prepared?

- Whenever you meet your manager, if you have a problem, do you always outline the answer you recommend? Are you able to mention the alternatives you have rejected, and your reasons, if asked?

- Do you hold regular informal meetings with your staff to avoid frequent and unnecessary interruptions?

- Do you insist that they must never bring a problem to you without having considered the available options and recommending a solution?

- Do you waste people's time by answering the telephone during informal meetings?

- Do you ask members of your team to come to your office without the courtesy of telling them your agenda?

- How often do you visit members of your team rather than have them visit you?

- Whenever someone telephones you to suggest a meeting, do you always ask the purpose and the priority needed?

- Whenever someone visits your office for an informal meeting, do you suggest another time if you are not sufficiently prepared or if it will interrupt a key task?

- Do your meetings always end with decisions approved or specific action and a deadline for completion agreed?

If you feel there is scope to improve your informal meetings, you must take action.

Effective formal meetings

Here are some tips to make your formal meetings more productive and use time more effectively.

Timing

There is no excuse for meetings which don't start on time and which don't finish by the scheduled time, or for people who arrive late. This wastes time and is sloppy management, and should be *stopped now*. Action you should take includes:

- getting everyone to agree that henceforth they will arrive by the scheduled time

- setting a personal example and expecting an apology to the meeting from anyone who arrives late

- scheduling meetings to finish either at lunchtime or at the end of the day, so that a failure to finish on time is likely to be unwelcome

- indicating at the start of the meeting which items are to be dealt with quickly

- not allowing anyone who has written a report to inform the meeting to waste time reading it aloud

Agenda

- Write or approve the agenda items yourself

- Do not waste time by including an item, 'approval of previous minutes', unless it is an official board meeting or suchlike

- place the most important item first and the least important one last. Then if time is short, you can still finish at the scheduled time and leave only the least important items not discussed

- Make the first item 'action not completed' and do not waste time by letting people describe irrelevant details and history of what they have done

- Prune the agenda so that it can be covered adequately within the scheduled time

- Make the agenda items sufficiently specific so people may prepare adequately

The agenda for regular monthly management meetings is often a recipe for time-wasting because it includes unchanging items such as marketing, sales, operations, product development, finance and personnel. For each meeting, specific items should be included on the agenda under each of these general headings. Always circulate the agenda, *and a complete and concise set of papers*, in sufficient time for people to arrive prepared.

Minutes

The two key essentials of an effective meeting are the agenda and the minutes. Writing minutes is too important a job to be delegated. So, action you should take includes:

- reducing the minutes to the absolute minimum, namely the action to be taken, the person accountable, and the completion date

- writing the 'action minutes' yourself during the meeting

- alternatively, at the end of each topic, dictating the 'action minute' to your personal assistant

- using the right-hand margin of the minutes as an action column; for example:

Action to be taken	Action by/ completion date
Prepare a draft mailshot for major distributors	PBH/2 Sept

- distributing the minutes within twenty-four hours so that no one has an excuse for not completing the action on time

Effective informal meetings

These require an equally disciplined approach as at formal meetings to achieve effective time management. So here are a few hints to help you.

Adopt 'MBWA'

This is shorthand for 'management by walking about'. 'And what exactly is that?' you might understandably ask.

It means that you make a regular habit of walking around to visit your team at their desks and hold brief, informal and disciplined meetings with people as appropriate. Some managers go walkabout at the start of each day they spend in the office. The benefits are:

- your team know when they can be sure to have a brief word with you

Management by walking about

- you see for yourself exactly what is happening

- you have the opportunity to maintain contact with every member of your team, and not just those who report directly to you

- you will reduce the number of interruptions by your staff substantially

Visit people

If you visit people in their offices, you can shorten the meeting by standing up to indicate you wish to conclude the meeting.

Hold standing meetings

When someone does visit you for an informal meeting, stand up to welcome them and *remain* standing. This indicates to people that it is to be a short meeting.

Take effective action now

Complete the action list for effective formal meetings and the one for informal meetings which follow. Write down, *in order of importance*, the improvements you will achieve three months from today for formal meetings and one month from today for informal meetings.

Effective formal meeting action list

List in order of importance:

Action to be taken   Person accountable
                                      /Completion date

1.

2.

3.

4.

5.

6.

Effective informal meeting action list

List in order of importance:

Action to be taken   Person accountable
                                       /Completion date

1.

2.

3.

4.

5.

6.

How to hold productive meetings – action checklist

By now, you will:

- have applied value analysis to both formal and informal meetings

- decide or approve the agenda for formal meetings you hold

- agree an agenda verbally at the beginning of every informal meeting

- have ensured your meetings start on time, finish by the scheduled time, and that the agenda is covered

- write action minutes during meetings and circulate them within twenty-four hours

- have adopted MBWA and hold informal meetings standing up in your office or, better still, visiting the person to speed up meetings and reduce interruptions

- have taken action to improve the formal meetings which you attend

8   HOW TO BECOME AN EFFECTIVE DECISION-MAKER

When you have read this chapter, *and implemented it*, you will:

- have identified which decisions need to be made to produce outstanding achievement

- make sure you address the fundamental result or opportunity

- consider the various options and alternatives open to you to avoid making blinkered decisions

- identify what could go wrong, assess the risks, and prepare contingency plans where appropriate

- overcome any tendency to procrastinate over or to delay making difficult decisions

- challenge the status quo constructively

Effective decision-making is straightforward, but the implementation may be difficult, risky or unpleasant. It is often the implementation involved which causes people to choose the easy option or to put off making a decision. One decision which is often delayed is the dismissal of someone reporting directly to you, because you have to handle the unpleasantness yourself. What is more, chief executives are just as guilty as anyone else at failing to handle difficult situations involving people effectively.

Assess your decision-making

Put your own decision-making to the test by completing the decision-making checklist which follows. It is designed to show the impact of your decision-making on the business.

Decision-making checklist

1.   List the most important decisions you have made and their impact:

This year

   Decision:
   Impact:

This month

   Decision:
   Impact:

This week

   Decision:
   Impact:

2.   List the most important decisions you need to make, and their impact:

                                      Deadline

This week

   Decision:
   Impact:

This month

   Decision:
   Impact:

This quarter

   Decision:
   Impact:

This year

   Decision:
   Impact:

Your action list will have revealed the importance of your decisions in terms of their impact on the company. To make sure that you are a really effective decision-maker, here are some proven methods.

Identify the major decisions

Outstanding achievement is extremely unlikely to result from only making the decisions which *have to be made*. Effective decision-makers:

- identify the decisions which, if made, will have the biggest impact on the key results

- identify any decisions which, if made, will achieve a quantum leap improvement in excess of the key results which have been set

- check with their manager and members of their team to ensure that the most important decisions to be made have been identified

Establish the fundamental purpose, result or opportunity

Whenever you are making a decision, and especially when a member of your team is making a recommendation for you to approve, ask the following questions:

- what result will be achieved?

- what is the fundamental purpose?

- what other options and opportunities should be explored?

'And,' you are saying to yourself, 'an illustration would be helpful.'
  Consider a routine decision in a small company. Your accountant

recommends recruiting a third accounts clerk to cope with expansion of the business:

- the result to be achieved is the handling of the increased volume of work

- the fundamental purpose is to meet the accounting needs of the business

- the other options available include:
    - eliminating and/or simplifying some of the work to remove the need to recruit
    - making available a junior person from within to handle filing
    - transferring 'non-accounting' work handled by the accounts department to other administrative departments with the capacity to cope without recruiting someone
    - combining elements from the above to eliminate the need to recruit
    - transferring someone from within the business to fill the vacancy, without the need to recruit a replacement
    - recruiting a part-time person instead of someone full-time
    - recruiting a junior filing clerk to enable the accounts clerks to concentrate on accounting work

- the other opportunities to be explored include:
    - having the payroll prepared by a computer bureau and eliminating the need for an extra accounts clerk
    - buying a microcomputer to replace the electromechanical book-keeping machine, which may eliminate the need to recruit or change the type of person to be recruited

Consider the owner of a substantial business who is in his late forties and preparing to retire within the next five years. He does not have any family wishing to help manage the business, but does have a strong management team, and is considering selling the company. The results to be achieved are:

- to enable the owner to retire or to reduce his involvement substantially within the next five years

- to have sufficient cash available to maintain his standard of living for the rest of his life

- to provide financial security for his wife if he dies first

- to make sure that the company continues successfully and that the staff keep their jobs

When major decisions are involved, make sure you define the various key results to be achieved. The other options available, in addition to an outright sale of the business to another company now, may include:

- selling the company on an 'earn-out' deal. This means that the owner sells some of the equity now, continues to manage the business, and agrees to sell the remainder of the equity at a given time, for a price related to the profits produced.

- selling the company to the existing management by a leveraged management buy-out, backed by a financial institution

- asking a financial institution to introduce a management team, with experience of the same industry, who want to buy a company with their financial backing

- recruiting or promoting someone to replace the owner as managing director. The owner will become non-executive chairman and continue to own the business

- selling, say, 25 per cent of the equity to a financial institution now, continuing to manage the business, and leaving other options still open

A major opportunity to be explored may be to obtain a stock exchange listing for the company as soon as possible and still retire when originally planned.

Keep yourself informed

Effective decision-makers are alert to which are the key decisions that should be made and which major opportunities should be explored because they keep themselves informed.

Complete the business development knowledge checklist which follows to make sure you keep yourself sufficiently well informed of what is happening in your industry.

Business development knowledge checklist

Do you:

Read the trade press regularly?

Scan the technical pages of relevant newspapers to look for developments which may affect your business?

Maintain links with relevant university research departments or industrial research associations?

Make sure you have the opportunity to meet major customers even if you are no longer directly involved in sales?

Visit the point of sale of your products occasionally, e.g., the wholesaler, retail outlet, or your own branch, to know what is happening?

Meet existing and potential suppliers occasionally to find out about their developments?

Visit the major exhibitions in your industry to keep informed about competitors?

Visit other countries expressly to meet overseas competitors, or to find new sources of supply, or to assess export opportunities, or to find out what is happening there at first hand?

Listen to your salespeople to keep yourself informed about your competitors?

Ask your customers about the opportunities and pressures facing them so that you can respond to their needs?

The business development knowledge checklist is not meant to be comprehensive; its purpose is to help you assess whether or not you keep sufficiently informed about your industry for effective decision-making.

Every member of the management team of a business, and any aspiring to join their ranks, should complete the checklist. Whatever your job – accountant, quality assurance manager, buyer, or distribution manager – business development knowledge gives insight and perspective to your decision-making.

So, take action now by completing the business development knowledge action plan which follows.

Business development knowledge action plan

Person and completion date

1. Action

2. Action

3. Action

4. Action

5. Action

Assess risks and prepare contingency plans

Effective decision-makers consciously think through the implementation of their decision. *To rehearse for success*, identify:

- what could go wrong
- obstacles you may face
- hostile responses by competitors, trade unions, consumer bodies or whoever

For each one, decide if it is sufficiently important to:

- assess the cost, damage and consequences
- plan to minimise or eliminate the risk in a cost-effective way
- develop contingency plans to minimise the consequences

Make small decisions in time

The need to make unpleasant decisions affecting members of your team can often be avoided by making small decisions early enough.

As a result of implementing the section of this book dealing with effective delegation, each member of your team will have agreed key results they should achieve and standards of performance they must maintain.

Whenever you see, or learn of, action or behaviour which falls short of the results and standards agreed you must *decide to tell the person immediately and privately*.

If you do not, then you are condoning mediocrity and are likely to create a more serious problem by your procrastination.

Take action *now*. Write down an action list of any unsatisfactory performance you need to tell a member of your team about. If you don't decide to tell them, you are doing them a disservice. Worse still, if you complain to your colleagues instead then you are doing the person an even bigger disservice.

Challenge the status quo constructively

Develop the habit of asking yourself, and encouraging members of your team to ask, why is it done or not done:

- at all?
- this frequently?
- to this standard?
- in this way?
- here?

'And,' you are saying to yourself, 'give some examples to get me thinking.' Here goes:

Why don't we offer a mail order service for those customers who find it inconvenient to visit our shops?

Why don't we create our own credit card as well as paying a charge to the major credit card companies when our customers use them?

Why don't we offer to arrange a mortgage for everyone who visits a branch of our estate agency, regardless of whether they buy or sell a house through us?

Why don't we use a computer database for direct response mailing shots to a target group of prospective customers?

Why don't we develop a version of our product to serve the particular needs of a given market segment and become the market leader in it?

Why do we buy our cars instead of using lease or hire purchase?

Why do we manage the staff catering facilities rather than use a specialist company?

Why do we have a large administrative staff located in expensive city centre offices?

To challenge the status quo constructively

Why do we   wait sixty days from the invoice date before asking the customer for payment?

Why do we   always type replies to internal memos when a handwritten reply on the original would often be appropriate?

To challenge the status quo constructively, however, requires that not only is the challenge made, but an improved alternative is developed as well.

How to become an effective decision-maker – action checklist

By now, you will

- have assessed the impact of your decision-making on the business
- have identified the major decisions you should make
- have established the fundamental purpose, result or opportunity before making a decision
- have prepared an action plan to keep you well informed of developments likely to affect your business sector
- assess risks and identify obstacles and reactions which you may face, and develop contingency plans
- challenge the status quo and develop improved methods

9 HOW TO DEVELOP PRESENTATION SKILLS TO SELL YOUR IDEAS

When you have read this chapter, *and implemented it*, you will:

- be convinced that presentation skills help you to achieve your success goals and manage your time effectively

- actively seek opportunities to develop your presentation skills

- feel confident about each presentation you are to make

- use visual aids effectively

- sell your ideas and recommendations to produce the results you want to achieve

The most powerful form of communication is face-to-face contact, because it enables you to convey conviction and enthusiasm as well as information.

Good presentation skills will enable you to communicate effectively, to sell your ideas and to achieve your success goals more quickly and easily in:

- informal conversations

- team meetings and briefings

- formal presentations

'And,' I hear you asking yourself, 'is there a winning approach I can adopt which suits all of these situations?' Yes!

Effective communication and presentation

There are six essential stages to effective communication and presentation:

- preparation
- attention
- interest
- desire
- conviction
- close

If you omit or mishandle any one of the six stages you risk failing to achieve the outcome you want, so consider these six essential stages in various situations.

Informal conversations

Preparation

Preparation is essential to get the results you want. So before the meeting:

- define the outcome you want as clearly as possible
- devise the 'informal agenda' to help achieve the desired outcome
- have the correspondence, paperwork, evidence and statistics you need to convince the other person
- identify the benefits for them, their department and the company
- summarise the financial justification for your case

Attention

- Telephone to agree when and where it will be convenient for the other person to meet you, so that he or she will have sufficient time available and be free from distractions and interruptions

- If the person is frequently interrupted by taking telephone calls in their own office, suggest using your office, a meeting room, or a breakfast, lunch or dinner meeting, as appropriate

- Do not start the conversation until you have obtained the person's complete attention

- If the person suggests you begin whilst he or she finishes reading incoming mail or signing correspondence, suggest you are happy either to wait a moment or to rearrange the meeting

Interest

- *Get to the point immediately, without waffling*

- Mention concisely the opportunities or results or issues to be discussed which will command attention

Desire

- Spell out the results and benefits for the person, their department and the company you want to achieve

Conviction

- convince them by outlining:
  - the financial justification
  - how it will work in practice
  - the tangible evidence to show it will work

- listen carefully to objections, doubts, queries and answer them succinctly

Get to the point immediately, without waffling

- respond positively to the person's ideas which are consistent with the outcome you want

Close

- close the conversation with agreement to the outcome you want

- agree *who* will do *what* by *when*

- if you do not get agreement to the outcome you want, ensure you agree positive action towards your goal

Team meetings and briefings

Preparation

Preparation is essential to demonstrate your own professionalism and your respect for your team. So before the meeting:

- define the outcome you want to achieve

- ensure you will have the support of key team members

- circulate an agenda and invite questions, comments and ideas on specific items where appropriate

- consider planning the meeting to end at lunchtime, so that the discussion can be continued informally during a buffet lunch

- ensure a suitable room and sufficient chairs will be available

- make sure that if coffee is to be served it is done in a way which avoids interruption or distraction

- prepare flip charts or acetate slides to convey facts and figures and to reinforce key points

Attention

- Insist that everyone should arrive promptly so that the meeting will start and finish on time

- Arrange for telephone messages to be taken so that no one is called away from the meeting

Interest, desire and conviction

- Use a combination of talking, listening, questions and discussion to maintain interest and to involve people

- Include some 'good news' stories such as recent success by the company and members of your team, individual promotions, expansion plans, and so on

- Focus on the sense of achievement, the benefits which will arise from the changes planned, and the need for action

Close

- close the meeting on a positive and motivating note

- summarise any changes which are to happen, and from what date they will become effective

- confirm any action which has been agreed during the meeting, and spell out *who has agreed to do what by when*

Formal presentations

These may be:

- to obtain approval of a major project by the group board

- at a company conference

- to a prospective customer to win a major order against competition

- on behalf of the company at a public seminar

In each of these situations you are an ambassador for yourself, your team and the company.

Preparation

Preparation is essential to ensure that you will be seen as an outstanding ambassador. So before the presentation:

- visit the venue to ensure you know how to get there on the day and to check the journey time

- inspect the room, check suitable power points are available, find out what seating layout will be used, and get the 'feel' of the room

- enquire how many people will be attending

- find out the type of audience to ensure your presentation is relevant, e.g. executive and non-executive directors; largely field salespeople, and a sprinkling of sales managers; mainly customers from the public sector

- arrange to receive an attendance list before your presentation

- agree the total time available to you, how long your presentation should last and the time to be allowed for questions and discussion

- rehearse your presentation to know how long it will take

- check that your slides will be suitable for the projection equipment available

- decide whether or not you wish to use a microphone and request the type you prefer

- if you are to be introduced, find out what will be said and ensure it is accurate and relevant

- if you are to follow another speaker, check that you will have time to test the equipment you will be using and set out things as you prefer them

- be sure that your visual aids can be seen clearly by everyone

Final preparation on the day of your presentation:

- listen to the last few minutes of the previous speaker, if possible, to assess the audience

- meet some of the delegates, even if only to shake hands, so you 'know' some of your audience and feel at home

- check the equipment is working and your material is in the correct sequence

- find out who will deal with any emergency such as projection equipment failure, microphone feedback or external noise

- *expect to be nervous and know your nerves will disappear within the first five minutes of your presentation*

Attention

- Make sure the audience is seated and ready for you to start *before you do start*

- Deliver your opening sentence crisply, reading it if necessary and *command their attention immediately*

Interest

- Remind people why the subject is important to them

- Tell them the topics you will cover, whether you welcome questions throughout or request people to reserve their questions, and how long your presentation will last

- What decision or approval you expect at the end, if appropriate

- Use either prepared flip charts or projector slides as visual aids

- Use key words on a set of cards or a photocopy of your projector slides to structure your presentation

- Don't read your presentation, because you will bore your audience

- Demonstrate your own conviction and enthusiasm by your words, tone of voice, gestures and facial expressions

- Spell out how they or the company will benefit

- Present factual evidence where appropriate rather than unsubstantiated opinions

- Demonstrate the financial justification for your case

- Illustrate how it works in practice

- Show that potential problems have been identified and overcome

- Invite questions and answer them authoritatively

Close

- Ask for the approval, order or action you want to conclude your presentation

Some general tips on using visual aids

- Use a comprehensive series of flipcharts or, better still, projector slides to structure your presentation for you and allow you to look at the audience whilst elaborating each point

- Present a minimum of essential information on each slide

- Restrict the content to twenty words or even fewer figures

- Realise that an ordinary typewriter doesn't produce large enough type to be seen clearly

- Make sure your slides are clearly numbered and in the correct sequence – any slip up will destroy your professionalism

- Use pictures, drawings and colour to add interest

- Use cartoons to add humour and to emphasise a point

Presentation style

- Entertain your audience and amuse them with anecdotes and illustrations

- Vary the tone and level of your voice to maintain interest

- Use jokes sparingly, unless the purpose of your presentation is primarily to entertain

- Avoid unnecessary risks such as using bad language, making sexist remarks, nationalist or racist comments, or jokes which could refer to any member of the audience

- Avoid excessive walking about or extravagant gestures

Take action *now*. Complete the presentation skills action checklist which follows to ensure you identify and implement the key actions which you need to make to improve your presentations.

Presentation skills action checklist

Informal Conversations

1.

2.

3.

Team Meetings and Briefings

1.

2.

3.

Formal Presentations

1.

2.

3.

How to develop presentation skills to sell your ideas action checklist

By now you will:

- use the six-stage approach for effective communications and presentations:
  - preparation
  - attention
  - interest
  - desire
  - conviction
  - close

- have made a presentation skills action checklist to improve the effectiveness of your:
  - informal meetings
  - team meetings and briefings
  - formal presentations

10 HOW TO WRITE EFFECTIVE BUSINESS PLANS, REPORTS, LETTERS AND MEMOS

When you have read this chapter, *and implemented it*, you will:

- produce convincing business plans

- write well-structured reports

- write clear, concise and effective letters

- spend less time writing

Most people leave school, college or university unable to write effectively for business. Too many people never attend a training course on effective writing early in their careers. Then they may be regarded as too senior to attend one, and have to rely on their own efforts to improve.

Avoid writing

People rightly complain about the mountain of paperwork they receive, but never stop to think what they could do to produce less paperflow themselves. Writing is *not* an effective way to communicate in terms of time management. Speaking is much quicker than writing, and so is dictation. Ways to avoid writing include:

- *not* confirming or acknowledging unless essential

- telephoning instead
- replying to internal memos with a handwritten note on the original
- using standard paragraphs where possible
- showing your personal assistant how to write routine letters
- only writing within your own team *if absolutely essential*

Don't confirm or acknowledge by letter

Before you dictate a letter to confirm a meeting or acknowledge receipt, ask yourself, 'Why it is essential to write a letter at all?'

- Instead of writing to confirm a meeting with someone, ask your personal assistant to telephone the day before just to check
- If the meeting is in your office, don't bother to confirm
- If you really do need to acknowledge receipt of a letter or report in writing, send a cryptic, one-line telex instead

Telephone instead of writing

It really is much quicker to telephone or, better still, have your personal assistant telephone to give your answer or to provide information, unless a two-line letter or telex will be sufficient.

Use the original to reply

For internal memos, it is appropriate to handwrite a cryptic reply on the original and return it.

Often the reply to a four-paragraph memo can be reduced to notes in the margin alongside the appropriate paragraph, e.g.:

Yes

by 21st Oct

57%

I'll speak to TH

Some managers only use this technique within their own division and only to people not senior to them. It is merely efficient time management to reply on the original, and is *not impolite*.

You should:

- reply on the original whenever appropriate to other divisions and subsidiaries in your group

- ask the Managing Director's personal assistant to confirm that he is happy to accept a reply handwritten on a memo from him. The answer is likely to be 'yes', and certainly should be.

Use standard paragraphs and sentences

Ask your personal assistant to compile a collection of paragraphs you use regularly, then to put them on the word processor and to index them. So when you are dictating a letter, you need simply say 'paragraph thirty-seven next' because you will have a copy of the standard paragraphs for reference.

A useful refinement is to use standard paragraphs with blank spaces to insert amounts, dates or reference numbers. Then you need simply dictate 'paragraph nineteen, £8,125, 10 August'.

Standard paragraphs can be especially useful for including as part of each 'individually written' sales proposal. 'And,' you are saying to yourself, 'please suggest some examples.'

Our aim is . . .

Our fees are . . .

Each curtain is made by . . .

Fitting is included . . .

Our terms of payment are . . .

It is paragraphs such as these which managers dictate regularly, and unnecessarily.

Don't write routine letters

As a manager, *it is not your job* to write routine letters. *Give the work away* to your personal assistant. Show her how to write routine letters if necessary by:

- dictating one of each type of routine letter as a 'basic model' for her to vary to suit the circumstances
- suggesting she creates her own library of routine letters and paragraphs on her word processor

Then all you need to do to write a routine letter is to handwrite on the original a note such as 'usual "not on shortlist" letter' and your personal assistant will do the rest.

Don't write within your team

Unless it is absolutely essential, don't write letters to members of your team and insist they don't as well.

Memos sent within a team smack of an impersonal and bureaucratic approach. Talk or telephone to the person instead.

Develop an effective writing style

Effective writing needs to be:

- clear
- understandable
- brief
- informal

Write clearly

Make the subject clear at the outset. Use a descriptive title, wherever possible, on memos and letters. For example:

Memo: Report on visit to Bankers Trust, London, on 22 February.
Letter:

Dear Mr Hayes
Request to increase mortgage

Use short sentences, simple words, and short paragraphs. Itemise individual points for clarity. For example:

Do not write: our performance in recent months has been adversely affected by the unusual climatic conditions.

Write instead: sales are 7 per cent below budget this quarter, mainly because of the poor summer weather.

Professional people, armed with a dictating machine, are amongst the worst offenders at writing longwinded sentences and paragraphs, which mean that clarity is reduced, the main point tends to get lost, and the punctuation may go astray; or worse still, the reader might lose interest and become bored, as this sentence of paragraph-like size should have demonstrated to you, if you have managed to reach the end of it!

Write understandably

Assess the background knowledge and level of understanding your readers have. Write accordingly, and avoid stating what they already know.

Beware of jargon that you don't even realise is jargon to people who don't work in either your industry or your company.

A business plan recently submitted to financial institutions contained jargon on two key items. The first-page summary simply described the business as 'the development, manufacture and sale of bus-standard software products adapted for marine applications' and went on to say 'profitability will improve significantly as the Cenman levy will not be payable'. Cenman was the group catchword for central management charges levied on each subsidiary, regardless of how much benefit it received.

Write briefly

Use words as if they are expensive, because they are expensive. Words take time to write, to read and to understand.

Write one- or two-line letters. Some examples of complete letters except for the name, address, subject and 'yours etc.' at the end are:

- We confirm our acceptance of the modification cost of £327, including VAT.

- Please provide a carousel projector, to take a Kodak slide holder, and a neck microphone.

- We confirm your reservation, as you requested, and look forward to welcoming you.

Write informally

Use the same words and expressions when you write as you do when speaking. Some examples showing *how not to write* make the point:

- We have received your letter dated the 4th December, quoting your reference C47/HL.

- You requested me to send you a suggested draft copy for the promotional literature and my first attempt is enclosed.

- We would like to propose the following basis for our working together, subject to our being mutually satisfied with the arrangements at the end of a three-month trial period.

These examples when written informally become:

- Thanks for your recent letter.

- The promotional 'blurb' you want is enclosed.

- The basis we propose, subject to review after three months, is . . .

Prepare to write efficiently

Efficient writing requires preparation. So:

- for letters and memos, jot down the points you wish to make 'in shorthand' and decide which order to put them in

- for a report or business plan, jot down the subject headings and put them in a logical order, and then list the points within each section

- have correspondence, files and statistics available before you start dictation

Write efficiently

Choose an efficient method to write:

- use a dictation machine rather than writing by hand, which takes much longer

- use some shorthand, if your personal assistant wishes to avoid losing some of her skill

- develop your keyboard skills to use for your own convenience and efficiency

Write with impact

Write with impact

When you are writing an internal report, *create impact* by starting with the recommendation or conclusion. In this way, readers have the opportunity merely to skim or to skip the detail as they feel appropriate.

When you are writing any long report, or business plan, make it easy to read:

- bind it properly
- include a contents page
- make the first page an executive summary
- number the pages
- use dividers so sections can be found quickly
- relegate supporting information to appendices
- avoid the need to turn the report through ninety degrees to read some pages

'And,' you are saying to yourself, 'exactly what do you mean by an executive summary?'

An executive summary should:

- highlight the recommendation, approval or action required
- outline the financial justification and benefits to be achieved
- be written on one side of paper
- be entirely understandable without reference to the remainder of the report
- summarise concisely every key item in the report

Always appeal for action

Always start and/or finish any plan, report, letter or memo by outlining the recommendation, approval or action you want from the reader.

If the recommendation, approval or action required of the reader is not spelled out, the likelihood of it happening will be reduced and so your writing will not be effective management of your time, because the work you did leading up to the report as well as the writing of it may simply fail to produce the result you wanted.

Take action *now*. Complete the effective writing action list which follows by writing down the key things you need to do to make your writing more effective.

If you are unsure what you need to improve, read critically some of the reports, letters and memos you have written recently before you write your action list. Do it today, however, whilst this chapter is still clearly in your mind.

Make a diary note a month from today to review some of your reports, letters and memos to ensure that your writing has become really effective.

Effective writing action list

Key actions to be taken to produce effective reports and business plans:

1.

2.

3.

4.

5.

Key actions to be taken to produce effective letters and memos:

1.

2.

3.

4.

5.

*How to write effective business plans, reports, letters and memos –
action checklist*

By now, you will:

- avoid writing whenever possible

- write with impact and always start and/or finish by appealing for
  the action you want

- write with a definite purpose to make a recommendation, obtain
  approval, or produce action

- write clearly, simply, concisely, informally

- have completed an action list to ensure you write effectively

11 HOW TO MANAGE THE TELEPHONE

When you have read this chapter, *and implemented it*, you will:

- use the telephone more effectively to produce results, get decisions approved and obtain action for you
- avoid unwelcome interruptions by the telephone
- make fewer abortive calls
- spend less time on the telephone

Manage your telephone, and don't let it manage you. Your telephone can be used effectively and save you time, or you can allow it to waste your time, cause you stress and continuously interrupt you and destroy your concentration. The choice is up to you.

'And,' you are saying to yourself, 'it is easier said than done, so how do I start?'

Incoming calls

You should not receive every telephone call simply because you are in your office, or worse still are somewhere in the building. You must ensure, however, that every incoming call is handled by someone or a message taken for action later.

You should not receive calls, *unless absolutely essential*, when you are:

- doing a selection, appraisal or disciplinary interview – because it is discourteous

- having an informal meeting with someone – because it wastes their time

- with a client or supplier – because it may appear unprofessional

- in a formal meeting – because it wastes everyone's time

Use your personal assistant to filter your incoming calls by ensuring she knows:

- only to interrupt you with emergency calls whenever someone is in your office

- not to transfer a call when you are in another person's office, unless specifically requested by you

- when you want to work on your own without any interruptions

- whom you wish to speak to when you are receiving calls

- to ask other callers for the purpose of their call, as well as their name and company

- to handle routine calls herself or to route them to one of your team whom she is sure will be able to answer

- to find out when it will be convenient to you and the caller for you to phone back

- to take a message so that you can phone back with an answer, instead of your having to call once to find out what the caller wants and then having to call again with the answer.

Outgoing calls

A few moments of preparation are essential to make effective and brief outgoing calls. Before dialling the number you should:

- be clear about the purpose of your call, in terms of the recommendation, approval or action required

Outgoing calls – a few moments of preparation are essential

- be sure you should be telephoning and not your personal assistant

- be ready to state the purpose of your call at the earliest possible moment

- have jotted down the key points you want to make

Before ending the call you should:

- confirm the recommendation, approval or action

- agree when it is mutually convenient for a return call to be made

Handle time-wasters effectively

Some people not only waste their own time and money when using the telephone, they will waste your time and money as well – it you let them. When you receive a call from a telephone time-waster, make them get to the point. Be ready to say things like:

- 'How can I help you?'

- 'I'm delighted to hear from you, although I have only five minutes to talk with you right now.'

Make calls to telephone time-wasters when they are likely to be either going home or to lunch. Still bring them to the point by saying something like:

- 'I am phoning you because . . .'

- 'I'm making a quick call because I have only five minutes.'

Avoid wasting your time

Even if you make brief and effective telephone calls, you can still waste your own time by:

- finding telephone numbers

- dialling numbers

- making abortive calls

Finding telephone numbers

Time spent finding telephone numbers can be largely eliminated by using a 'memory telephone'. Telephones are readily available which will store forty numbers, and this will be sufficient to handle perhaps 80 per cent of the outgoing calls you make.

For other numbers, your personal assistant should make a telephone database for you, and continuously make additions, deletions, and amendments. The format could be:

- a telephone book, small enough to carry in your briefcase

- a card index for your desk

- using a screen in your office

Dialling numbers

A memory telephone will largely eliminate time wasted by dialling numbers yourself. A recall facility will re-dial engaged numbers when you press a single button.

Using your personal assistant to dial numbers for you may be effective time management if:

- you give her several numbers to obtain, rather than interrupting her several times

- you have other work to do whilst you are waiting for her to obtain your numbers

137

Avoid making abortive calls

To avoid making abortive phone calls to people you telephone often:

- find out which days of the week and what time of the day you are most likely to be able to contact them

- tell them when you are most likely to be available to receive calls from them

Whenever you make an abortive call, always agree when it will be mutually convenient to make a return call, or ask for the answer to be phoned to your personal assistant.

Take action *now*. Complete the effective telephone action list which follows.

Effective telephone action list

Key action to be taken for effective telephone action:

Incoming calls:
1.

2.

3.

4.

5.

Outgoing calls:
1.

2.

3.

4.

5.

How to manage the telephone – action checklist

By now, you will:

- receive only emergency calls when you are engaged in a discussion or meeting

- ensure your personal assistant makes and receives telephone calls for you whenever appropriate

- know the purpose of your call and jot down key points before telephoning

- make telephone time-wasters get to the point quickly

- avoid wasting your time by finding numbers and dialling unnecessarily

- minimise abortive calls by knowing when to phone regular contacts

- have written an effective telephone action list to implement

12 HOW TO INCREASE YOUR OWN PRODUCTIVITY

When you have read this chapter, *and implemented it*, you will:

- action your in-tray more effectively

- read more quickly

- reduce time spent filing

- use travel time more effectively

- make better use of electronic information technology

- set standards which are *sufficient for the purpose*

Action your in-tray effectively

Remember the expression 'he sits there simply wasting his time by shuffling his papers'. This sums up a failure to deal with the in-tray effectively. To handle your in-tray effectively you must:

- stop unwanted items reaching you

- throw away your in-tray

- handle nearly everything only once

- deal with your incoming mail in a batch

Stop unwanted items

An important step in cutting down your in-tray to a manageable size is to stop unwanted items reaching you. Items unwanted by you may include:

- unsolicited 'free' magazines
- things which your predecessor wanted
- junk mail
- regular reports and printouts
- the whole report when you only need the summary
- copy correspondence which some people send you regularly
- mail which should be directed to another department for action
- routine items which should be actioned by your personal assistant

So, ask your personal assistant to:

- open the mail instead of you
- scrap junk mail
- remove your name from the circulation list of unwanted magazines
- re-route mail which should be handled by another department
- distribute mail directly to members of your team wherever appropriate
- remove your name from unwanted internal circulation lists
- sort the incoming mail you receive

An effective way for your personal assistant to sort mail is into:

- mail addressed to one of your team which you need to be aware of, for example a customer complaint, but which should be actioned by someone else
- any item which must be actioned by you urgently

- other items needing replies or action
- things for information only

Handle things only once

Handle your incoming mail only once, as follows:

- With mail you decide should be actioned by someone else, handwrite any comment needed and re-route it
- With correspondence needing a reply, batch process it, as described below
- With mail for information only, either dump it, or scan and dump it, or place in your 'to be read' folder
- With items which merit considerable time, place it in your 'to action' folder

In this way, you will process your incoming mail on the day you receive it. Sorting through your in-tray will have become a thing of the past.

Your 'to action' folder should contain only a handful of important items requiring action by you.

Your 'to be read' folder should be something you only look at when you have 'spare time' or a few minutes between meetings, or whatever. When you open it, still use the scan and dump approach.

Batch-process correspondence

The most efficient way to handle correspondence is in a batch. If you dictate your replies to your personal assistant, she will appreciate the reduced number of interruptions by you. To dictate effectively:

- have the original correspondence in a batch
- jot down on the original the key points to be made, where necessary
- dictate only your reply and give the original to your personal assistant so she can address the correspondence correctly.

Read more quickly

Computers and word processors have increased the number and size of reports produced, and so the amount of reading to be done by managers has increased.

Speedreading is worthwhile. You may feel that you need to take a two-day course on speedreading. Before you decide to spend that much time and money, consider the key techniques for fast and effective reading.

Fast and effective reading requires you to:

- preview long reports
- avoid sub-vocalising
- scan and skip
- cope with figures
- use a highlighter pen

Preview long reports

Don't read the report from start to finish initially. Preview it instead, by reading:

- the executive summary, if there is one
- the conclusion or recommendation
- any graphs or charts

In this way you will have digested the key features of the report and, by quickly flicking through the pages, will know which sections are of little or no interest to you.

Avoid sub-vocalising

People tend to read slowly by voicing the words silently to themselves, instead of reading quickly with their eyes. So you need to:

- check whether or not you sub-vocalise

- keep your eyes moving forward all of the time, *not* forwards and backwards

- try placing your finger under the centre of each line and move it down the page rapidly to pull your eyes along

Scan and skip

Any report, however well it has been written, will contain some sentences, paragraphs, pages, and sections which are either of little value to you or are irrelevant for your purpose and needs. So ensure you develop the habit of:

- scanning rather than reading as soon as you reach even a sentence of less relevance for you

- skipping, and not reading at all, anything which is irrelevant for your purpose

Cope with figures

Many people find that their speedreading techniques come unstuck when they are confronted with a schedule of figures or a computer printout, but this should not be allowed to happen to you.

When reading a schedule of figures, get into the habit of:

- first, reading the headings across the top

- next, reading the lines down the side

- then rapidly deciding which are the key figures you need and looking at them

- if the key figures are uncontentious, not bothering with the rest

- checking any notes at the bottom of the page to be aware of any important qualification about the figures

145

If one of the key figures is unsatisfactory or looks unusual, scan the column in which it occurs to find out what the cause is.

Before you open a computer print-out, decide exactly what you need to get from it. You need to be quite specific. For example, from a debtor print out you may only wish to know:

- any customer owing more than his credit limit

- any customer owing more than £1,000 over ninety days

So you should:

- ask if a summary can be prepared to show only the information you require

- if this is not possible, simply ask your personal assistant to scan the appropriate columns and mark the figures you need to look at

Use a highlighter pen

Highlighter pens are not a gimmick. Highlighter pens are an essential and inexpensive tool for effective time management.

Whenever you read reports and correspondence, have a highlighter pen in your hand to highlight key words, phrases, figures and points to action.

Then you can read the highlighted words and figures of a report again in a fraction of the time needed to reread the whole report, even if you use speedreading to do it.

Reduce filing

Some things *must* be filed. A lot of things, however, are filed unnecessarily.

You should regard filing as a total waste of your time, and as a potential waste of time for your personal assistant. The more things you file, the more difficult it is to find what you want.

For effective information storage you should:

- use the waste paper basket whenever possible – *be ruthless*
- add an address to your database, rather than file a letter
- set up central files for your team, so that only one copy is stored
- insist that filing is done daily, to save work
- ensure that correspondence is filed in date order
- keep bulky reports and brochures in a separate section of each file
- dump whole files whenever appropriate
- archive completed files which must be stored – but purge them of unwanted items first

Use travel time effectively

Managers spend a considerable amount of time travelling, so travel should be avoided whenever possible and necessary travel made as productive as possible.

Business travel falls into three categories:

- to and from work
- within your own country
- overseas

Travel to and from work

Many managers spend ten hours or more travelling between home and work each week. The cost of housing may prohibit you from living nearer to your work, so it is important to make your travelling time productive. So, consider changing your travel habits by:

- driving outside peak hours to shorten your journey
- travelling by train, using first class

First-class rail travel to and from work is neither a luxury nor an ego trip. It allows you to use your time effectively to:

- read the financial and trade press
- action your 'to read' file
- plan your diary for the day
- read management books and articles

Travel within your own country

Whilst face-to-face communication is invaluable, it often requires time-consuming travel. So, you should:

- make sure the purpose to be achieved justifies a meeting
- use teleconferencing and conference telephone facilities wherever appropriate
- arrange meetings in your offices, or in a convenient hotel to minimise travel
- use the train or a driver so that you can use the travel time for reading, telephoning and dictating

Travel overseas

Some people manage to work on planes, but many find it difficult and understandably so. Overseas business travel is exciting to start with but quickly becomes an essential chore. So make sure:

- the time you will spend away from your office contributes sufficiently to your key results to make the journey worthwhile

- your itinerary and appointments are planned before you set off

- each person you are to visit knows the purpose of your visit when you arrange it

Then the important thing is to arrive as fit for work as possible by:

- adopting the local meal and sleeping times during your flight

- avoiding any excess of food or alcohol

- drinking plenty of water to counter the effects of dehydration

- recognising that jetlag does exist and allowing sufficient time to recover from long flights before important meetings such as acquisition or contract negotiations

Benefit from information technology

Take a short cut. Talk to an expert, or at least someone with relevant experience such as:

- the director of information technology in your company

- your data processing or finance staff colleagues

- equipment suppliers at information technocomputer exhibitions

Find out the things which they feel are likely to be most productive for you and your team. Possibilities include:

- a microcomputer – for spreadsheet analysis, financial modelling, data base access

- desk top publishing – for professional-looking reports and manuals

- on-line data base information services – for effective desk research

- teleconferencing – as an alternative to travelling to meetings

- electronic mail boxes – for efficient communication

Benefit from information technology

- remote banking services – for electronic funds transfer

By the time this book is published, no doubt other developments will be available. So continue to keep yourself informed by talking to experienced information technology users whenever you have the opportunity.

Set relevant standards

There is little merit, if any, in pursuing perfectionism.

Effective time management requires that the standards set are sufficient for the purpose. Excessively high standards, for the particular purpose, are a costly indulgence.

Whilst the highest standards of presentation should apply for customer correspondence and reports, the following standards are sufficient internally:

- handwritten figures on schedules and reports

- a handwritten reply on the original correspondence

- stapled copies of reports rather than expensive binding

- free use of vending machines instead of expensive catering services

- figures expressed only to the nearest thousand for ease of calculation, typing, checking and reading.

Take action now. Complete the personal productivity action list which follows. List only the actions which will save you a worthwhile amount of time.

Personal productivity action list

Key action to improve personal productivity:

In-tray:

Reading:

Filing:

Travel:

Electronic equipment:

Relevant standards:

How to improve your own productivity – action checklist

By now you will:

- have stopped unnecessary correspondence reaching you

- have thrown away your in-tray

- use the most effective speedreading techniques

- have reduced filing to the essential minimum

- use travelling time for productive work

- have found out specific ways that information technology can improve your productivity

- ensure that your standards are not too high for the purpose

13 HOW TO USE YOUR DIARY TO MANAGE TIME

When you have read this chapter, *and implemented it*, you will:

- plan your day, week, month, and especially your year to action key tasks effectively

- have meeting-free days to give you flexibility

- have scheduled 'open door' and 'management by walking about' times to maintain personal contact with your team

- enable people to reach you by phone

- have a daily action list to get things done promptly

- use an effective follow-up system to make sure things happen on time

'And,' you are saying to yourself, 'if only this chapter can deliver all of this for me.' Well, it will.

Plan your time effectively

There is an old expression, 'Take care of the pennies, and the pounds will look after themselves.' Unfortunately, many managers seem to adopt a similar approach to time management. They assume that by creating a 'plan for today' each morning the key tasks which will produce the key results which will realise the success goals will get done. Wrong, it is too fragmented an approach.

Effective time management requires you to plan your:

- year

- months

- weeks

- days

Plan your year first . . . and your day last

It is much easier than you think. Enter into your diary for the rest of the year:

- **Regular meetings** – such as board meetings, monthly management meetings, short weekly meetings, etc.

- **Known one-off events** which you need to attend such as annual sales conferences, the annual general meeting with shareholders, visits to trade exhibitions, budget review meetings, etc.

- **Holidays** – make sure you take your full entitlement because it is an investment in your health, and effective time management.

- **Family occasions** – plan now to leave early for your wedding anniversary, and your spouse's and children's birthdays. Telephone schools to find out when sports days, speech days and parents' evenings take place. Find out from any children at university when graduation day is to be held. To achieve balance in your life, it is important to make time for your family on the occasions which are important to them.

- **Key tasks** – reserve sufficient whole days specifically for the key tasks which will produce the key results which will deliver outstanding achievement.

Depending upon your job, key tasks may be to:

- have a two-day strategic workshop with your team

Plan your year first . . . and your day last

- prepare the annual budget

- visit the Far East to find new sources of supply

- ensure you do spend some time each month visiting major customers, potential suppliers or whomever

It is essential to reserve time now for the known events and the key tasks, otherwise your time is likely to be consumed by seemingly urgent trivia each day. As soon as you get your new diary each year, plan the whole year. It doesn't matter that you don't know who you should visit in the Far East this far ahead of your visit, what is important is that you reserve the time to make a three-week trip if you feel this is needed.

Likewise, you are not deciding which major customers or potential suppliers to visit, you are simply reserving the time to be able to visit them.

Plan your next month

Now that you have planned the known events and key tasks for the year, take stock of your diary for next month by counting up how many 'equivalent full days' remain unplanned. You may well be shocked by how little time remains. If so, it is important to:

- avoid any temptation to 'cancel' days reserved for key tasks, because this will either delay or deny outstanding achievement, unless you can delegate them effectively now

- make sure you attend the important events

- ask yourself which of the regular meetings you will either cancel or not attend

Remember, regular meetings mortgage your time. Review each of your regular meetings again by asking:

- what worthwhile results and action are produced

- how few people need meet for how short a time to produce the results and actions needed

- how infrequently the meetings should be held

Key tasks – reserve sufficient whole days

Plan the next month by reserving at least one meeting-free day each week, so that you will be able to use these days either to concentrate on key tasks, working at home if necessary, or to arrange a full-day visit at short notice. Some people are hardly ever able to make a full-day visit with less than two or three weeks' notice, despite a real need or benefit to do so sooner, because they allow each day to be broken up by at least one meeting.

Reserve time for short-term key tasks. For example, make sure you will have sufficient time available when it is necessary to:

- hold selection interviews as a result of the job advertisement you placed in the newspaper

- write a particular report

- make a brief overseas visit to a major customer later this month

Plan this week

Make effective weekly time management habits work for you. Decide when you will:

- hold a regular and short team meeting, if necessary by having a sandwich lunch together

- make a point to be available to receive incoming telephone calls so that people know when they are more likely to be sure of contacting you.

For example, you may decide to make a habit every week, unless a major event or crisis intervenes, to have a sandwich lunch with your team each Friday and then work in your office that afternoon so that your people know that you are likely to be available to receive phone calls.

Whichever weekly time management habits you adopt, enter them in your diary now for the rest of the year. Otherwise, urgent trivia are likely to prevent you from ever acquiring effective time management habits.

Plan each day at the outset

Make effective daily time management habits work for you. Plan your day at the outset and decide when to:

- Go 'MBWA', management by walking about, and/or have an 'open door' period

- spend time with your personal assistant

- dictate correspondence and memos

- arrange meetings

Get into the habit of planning your day at the outset. If you travel by train or are driven to work, plan your day while you are travelling. If you drive to work, it is essential to arrive before people and telephone calls begin to interrupt you so that you can plan your day. If you allow your day to start unplanned, it is likely to end that way, and you will go home feeling, 'I've been really busy all day and I don't seem to have accomplished anything.'

It is *not* efficient time management to have an open door policy all day long. This literally invites people to interrupt you whenever they choose. Instead, consider going 'MBWA' first thing every morning and/or having an open door period from, say, five o'clock each day. By this time of day, people are more likely to want to be brief so that they can go home.

Arrange to spend time with your personal assistant and do your dictation as soon as possible after you receive your mail, so that your assistant knows her priorities for the day and can ensure that mail is despatched the same day as you dictate it.

Ask your personal assistant to set the starting times of meetings so that there will be a subtle pressure on people to want to finish them by lunchtime or the normal office closing time. When you need or want to spend time with someone who is reluctant to give you sufficient interruption-free time for discussion, ask your assistant to suggest a breakfast, lunch or dinner meeting.

Make daily action lists

Each morning, as part of planning your day at the outset:

- list the jobs to be done today

- list the phone calls you need to make

- avoid undue pressure on yourself by writing a number against each one to indicate the sequence which will ensure the most important things are done first

Follow up effectively

Some people attempt to use a 30-day follow-up file, but quite often the routine breaks down. Use a simpler and more effective system.

Ask your personal assistant to set up only three follow-up files:

- this week

- next week

- this month

Whenever you decide something needs to be followed up, simply mark the letter or memo T/W, N/W or T/M and your assistant will put it into the appropriate file. Then she should adopt another effective time management habit which will work for you.

Every Friday morning she will follow up as many items as possible in the 'this week' file, give you any needing action by you, and transfer the contents of the 'next week' file into the 'this week' file in readiness for next Friday.

On the last Monday morning of each month she will take follow-up action on the items in the 'this month' file.

Choose an effective system

The shortcoming of annual diaries is that they are not designed for effective time management. So visit a shop which stocks a wide range of diary systems and choose one allowing you to plan each day in 30-minute units, and list the phone calls and things to be done.

The following illustration shows the type of diary page you should look for and how to use it for effective time management.

A preferred diary format

08.00		**Thursday, 7 October**
08.30	*Breakfast with JPH*	Things to be Done
09.00	*MBWA*	*dictate BA*
09.30	*PA/dictation*	*visit report* 2
10.00		*approve budget*
10.30		*timetable*
11.00		1
11.30		*See Paul*
		re Falcon discount
12.00	*Visit Bankers Trust*	3
12.30		
13.00	*Sandwich lunch with team*	
13.30		Phone Calls to Make
14.00	*key task work*	*RCB- re Enfield 3*
14.30	*new brochure format*	*Frank Purkis 4*
15.00		*Geoff Tustain 1*
15.30		*Janice Long, BT2*
16.00		
16.30		
17.00		
17.30	*open door and things*	
18.00	*to be done*	
Evening		
	8·00pm Squash with PAB	

Take action *now*. Complete the effective diary action list which follows.

Effective diary action list

Key action to: Complete by

Purchase a suitable diary system

Plan next year and month

Adopt effective weekly time management habits

Adopt effective daily time management habits

Set up a follow-up system

How to use your diary to manage time – action checklist

By now, you will:

- plan your year first, then each month, week and day – to make sure the key tasks are completed on time

- create a daily plan before you do anything else – to ensure every day is productive for you

- have adopted weekly and daily effective time management habits – to become more accessible to people and suffer less interruptions

- use an efficient follow-up system – to ensure effective delegation and that deadlines are met

14 SUMMARY

Now that you have *implemented* this book, you should have:

Set your sights on outstanding success, and . . .

- Adopted the quantum leap approach to set your sights high and to achieve demanding goals.

- Defined your success goals to focus on the important things to be achieved; set three-year and one-year success goals; identified sub-goals to be achieved to ensure your success.

- Written down why you believe you will succeed in order to identify why your success goals are important to you, why they are achievable, what obstacles may have to be overcome and what priorities you need to focus on.

- Recognised the importance of achieving balance in your life by finding time to do things for your health and your relationships with family and friends.

Improved your time management, and . . .

- Have ranked your key results to be achieved.

- Have identified and ranked the major opportunities.

- Created action lists to give away routine work and to focus on the key tasks you need to handle for outstanding achievement.

- Helped your secretary to become a valuable personal assistant.

- Received only emergency calls when you are engaged in a discussion or meeting.

- Ensured your personal assistant makes and receives telephone calls for you whenever appropriate.

- Have stopped unnecessary correspondence reaching you.

- Have thrown away your in-tray.

- Used the most effective speed-reading techniques.

- Have found specific ways that information technology can improve your productivity.

Created the image of success, and . . .

- Have made your appearance and office already reflect the achievement of your success goals.

- Have begun to rehearse for success; imagining, thinking and acting now as if you had already achieved your success goals.

Created an outstanding team to help achieve your success goals, and . . .

- Listed the external and internal obstacles to success and written down how you will overcome them.

- Identified, developed and evaluated major opportunity proposals.

- Identified the recruitment you need to make to ensure outstanding achievement.

- Written an action plan to create and maintain excitement amongst your team.

- Checked that you really do delegate effectively.

- Made a habit of saying thank you every time for a job well done.

- Written a personal training and development plan for each person reporting to you, and for yourself.

Held effective meetings, and . . .

- Have applied value analysis to both formal and informal meetings.

- Decided or approved the agenda for formal meetings you hold.

- Agreed an agenda verbally at the beginning of every informal meeting.

- Written action minutes during meetings and circulated them within 24 hours.

- Have adopted MBWA and held informal meetings standing up in your office or, better still, visited the person to speed up meetings and reduce interruptions.

Become an effective decision maker, and . . .

- Have identified the major decisions you should make.

- Have established the fundamental purpose, result or opportunity before making a decision.

- Assessed risks and identified obstacles and reactions that you may face and developed contingency plans.

Made effective presentations, and . . .

- Used the six-stage approach for effective communications and presentations:
  - preparation
  - attention
  - interest
  - desire
  - conviction
  - close

Written purposefully, and . . .

- Avoided writing whenever possible.

- Written with impact and always started and/or finished by appealing for the action you want.

- Written with a definite purpose to make a recommendation, obtain approval, or produce action.

- Written clearly, simply, concisely, informally.

Managed your diary effectively, and . . .

- Planned your year first, then each month, week and day – to make sure the key tasks are completed on time.

- Created a daily plan before you do anything else – to ensure every day is productive for you.

COMMON-SENSE TIME MANAGEMENT

- Have adopted weekly and daily effective time management habits – to become more accessible to people and suffer fewer interruptions.

INDEX

INDEX

The Mercury titles on the pages that follow may also be of interest.
All Mercury books are available from booksellers or, in case of
difficulty, from:

Mercury Books
Gold Arrow Publications Ltd
862 Garratt Lane
London SW17 0NB

Further details and the complete catalogue of Mercury business
books are also available from the above address.

Also by Barrie Pearson . . .

COMMON-SENSE BUSINESS STRATEGY

How to improve your profits and cash flow dramatically.

Millions of managers and business owners have read books or attended seminars on strategy. Few people actually do manage their business strategically and they tend to have become millionaires!

Planning techniques have become so complicated that they are the preserve of 'planning experts'. The result has been long-winded business plans filed and forgotten almost as soon as they have been written.

Successful managers use strategic common-sense, not complex planning techniques. *Common-Sense Business Strategy* shows you how to create your own success story by achieving a 'quantum jump' improvement in results.

This book is based on more than ten years' successful experience of advising businesses ranging from household-name multinationals to unquoted companies and professional partnerships. *Common-Sense Business Strategy* tells you what to do, how to do it, and where to start. It is a book for those who want to manage strategically, and not simply read about it.

Common-Sense Business Strategy reveals . . .

- **How to Manage Strategically, using Common Sense**
- **How to Lay the Foundations for Success**
- **How to Take Stock of your Market Place**
- **How to Take Stock of your Company's Performance**
- **How to Develop a Vision to Ensure Success**
- **How to Overcome Obstacles to Success**
- **How to Develop Major Alternatives**
- **How to Make Successful Acquisitions**
- **How to Turn Around Loss-making Companies**
- **How to Hold a Strategic Workshop**
- **How to Make the Vision become Reality**
- **How to Make Successful Management Buy-outs and Buy-ins**

ISBN 1–85251–050–1   £14.95

WHO CARES WINS

How to unlock the hidden potential in people at work . . . and turn ordinary companies into winners.

By Peter Savage, with foreword by Sir John Egan

Today's winner is without question the company that shows how to utilise the men and women at its disposal more effectively than its competitors can utilise theirs. In *Who Cares Wins*, a practical guidebook to modern management, Peter Savage draws on his own extensive experience to explain how anyone can master the art of group motivation. His step-by-step outline of the key to effective man-management looks at the problems and challenges confronting modern managers and supervisors at every level from the chief executive down, and considers how recent theories of 'excellence' can be transformed into practical and profitable reality.

Savage looks in detail at the right ways and wrong ways of approaching personal relationships at work. He explains how to create a platform for change, then looks at how it can be used, with spectacular results, to unlock unexpected extra energy from colleagues and employees. He identifies this crucial hidden energy as 'discretionary potential' – that piece of ourselves we all take to work but more often than not don't bother to apply. We all know already there are more effective ways of working within organisations large and small: *Who Cares Wins* is the story of how to achieve them.

ISBN 1–85252–015–9   £6.99

IF ONLY I HAD SAID . . .
Conversation control skills for managers

By Charles Margerison

How can you become more effective in your relationships with others? You can start by knowing how to control conversations.

What you say and how you say it is a key to success. This is particularly so when you are in a managerial position responsible for getting a team of people to work together. Business conversations can be won or lost depending on how you communicate. The techniques for success depend on recognising cues and clues, signs and signals, assumptions and assertions along with other key messages.

This book teaches you how to respond effectively using time dynamics, problem and solution-centred behaviour, requests and statements, and other methods such as parallel and sequential conversation.

This is the manager's handbook of how to become more effective in your dealings with people. It enables you to get your message across and understand others more quickly. You will be able as a result to get more done in less time – and what you do will be accepted and more effectively implemented than before.

The book is based on years of practical work with managers. The case examples illustrate practical uses in sales, production, personnel, research, marketing and training. Special exercises are provided for you to assess your own conversation control skills.

ISBN 1–85252–012–4   £5.99

CALL YOURSELF A MANAGER!

By Matthew Archer

Throughout the business world there are thousands of people trying desperately hard to become 'a manager'. Some of those who have made it to a management position have aspirations of becoming the 'chief executive'. It is not too difficult to acquire the technical knowledge that goes with the job but the human element is much more elusive: managers, being human, are subject to their own weaknesses and their performance can be affected by their fears, prejudices, lifestyle and relationships with others.

In this book, based on long experience (the examples are real – if disguised) the author analyses a wide range of management styles. In an amusing and readable manner, the author gives busy managers useful and practical advice on how to improve their performance and how to make both their own working lives and those of their staff more enjoyable and productive.

ISBN 1–85252–000–0   **£4.95** (paperback)

STRESS MANAGEMENT TECHNIQUES

Managing people for Healthy Profits.

By Dr Vernon Coleman

In an average lifetime the average employee loses one and a half years from work because of stress-induced illness. The result is that stress costs British industry £20,000,000,000 a year – far more than is lost through strikes or industrial disputes.

'Britain,' says Dr Vernon Coleman, 'leads the world in expensive, stress-induced disease.' He points out that if a company employs just 100 people then stress will cost that company around £400 a day. In a company which employs 1,000 people stress costs £1,000,000 a year.

Whatever else you try, and however much you spend on equipment, nothing will improve your company's efficiency and profitability more than taking care of your employees and reducing their unnecessary exposure to stress.

In *Stress Management Techniques* Dr Vernon Coleman explains exactly how, why and when stress causes problems. More importantly, he also explains exactly how you can control and minimise the amount of stress in your company.

Stress Management Techniques is illustrated with case histories and packed with easy-to-follow practical advice.

There have been many books about stress before. This book is unique in that it explains exactly how you can keep stress in your company to a minimum.

ISBN 1–85251–036–6   £9.95